T0285974

DREAMER

DREAMER

MY LIFE ON THE EDGE

NAZEM KADRI

WITH DAN ROBSON

VIKING

VIKING

an imprint of Penguin Canada, a division of Penguin Random House Canada Limited

Canada • USA • UK • Ireland • Australia • New Zealand • India • South Africa • China

First published 2024

www.penguinrandomhouse.ca

All images courtesy of the author unless otherwise stated.

LIBRARY AND ARCHIVES CANADA CATALOGUING IN PUBLICATION
Title: Dreamer : my life on the edge / Nazem Kadri.
Names: Kadri, Nazem, author.
Identifiers: Canadiana (print) 2024033356X | Canadiana (ebook) 20240333578 |
ISBN 9780735247772 (hardcover) | ISBN 9780735247789 (EPUB)
Subjects: LCSH: Kadri, Nazem. | LCSH: Hockey players—Canada—Biography. |
LCSH: Muslim athletes—Canada—Biography. | LCGFT: Autobiographies.
Classification: LCC GV848.5.K33 A3 2024 | DDC 796.962092—dc23

Book design by Matthew Flute
Cover design by Matthew Flute
Cover image © Kevin Sousa / Getty Images
Typeset by Sean Tai

Printed in the United States of America

10 9 8 7 6 5 4 3 2 1

Penguin
Random House
VIKING CANADA

CONTENTS

1. A Long Line of Grinders   1
2. Growing Out of My Prom Suit   13
3. A Scrawny Kid Among Men   19
4. Home-Ice Advantage   30
5. Three Generations in Montreal   39
6. Learning to Celly   45
7. "Game On"   53
8. Getting Ahead of Myself   61
9. Still Grinding   69
10. A Movie I'll Never Watch   78
11. Finding My Game   84
12. "A Very Winnable Series"   98
13. An Opportunity My Grandfather Never Had   109
14. Aftermath   117
15. Great Teammates, Bad Team   126
16. Proving It   136
17. A New Era Begins   145
18. Skills There Are No Trophies For   154
19. Bad Decisions for Good Reasons   168

20. Finding Out the Hard Way   176
21. New Beginnings   183
22. Where It All Came Together   197
23. Shuffling on the Edges   214

    Acknowledgments   219
    Index   221

1
A LONG LINE OF GRINDERS

I SHUFFLED IN MY SKATES, searching for balance. Another cold and crowded day, but I was on the ice again—and on the ice I was happy. Skating brought the promise of warmth. It meant hands clutching a cup of steaming hot chocolate and the heat of my father beside me. We'd often visit the outdoor rink at Victoria Park in downtown London, Ontario; it was one of my favourite places to be. And it was a free skate, which meant a chance to practise the art my father and I had watched on television.

I pictured myself raising a silver trophy high above my head, just as those grown men had.

In London, most hockey fans support either the Toronto Maple Leafs, the Detroit Red Wings, or the Buffalo Sabres, the city having a nearly equal proximity to each team.

But we loved the Montreal Canadiens.

My dad became a Habs fan when he was young, shortly after he arrived in Canada from Lebanon when he was five years old. At first he was drawn to the team's jerseys—he loved the logo and the sharp red and blue colours. It was the 1970s, when the Canadiens were the best team in hockey, with players like Guy Lafleur, Serge Savard, and Larry Robinson. Dad learned the game watching the dynasty that won five Cups in a decade, including four straight.

It was hard to argue with my father's allegiances. The Canadiens won the Stanley Cup for him again in 1986. Then I came along. One of my first memories is of the Habs winning the Cup in 1993, when I was three.

Early on, my parents saw how much I enjoyed practising my hockey moves—whether it was at Victoria Park or one of the dozens of indoor arenas across London—so they found ways to make sure I could learn. And for my father, it was a chance to share a game he loved. We pursued it together.

Saturday nights were our nights, our bonding time. We'd watch *Hockey Night in Canada* together every week, and would catch the highlights of every game. It's one of the fondest memories of my childhood—just Dad and I sitting on the couch together, watching hockey.

As I grew, the game became a constant part of my life.

I remember playing hockey outside on the street, as young as three or four years old, in my running shoes with a tiny stick in my hands. And each winter I'd help my father build a rink in our backyard, handing him the tools and pretending to do my part. Then, when I was old enough, I joined minor hockey, practising and playing several times a week. I was a short and skinny kid, usually one of the smallest on my team. I was skilled, but never the best player on the ice.

In many ways, my childhood was similar to that of most of my minor hockey teammates. They all had parents who drove them to skate at Victoria Park, or helped them build a rink in their backyard, or shuttled them around town to games and practices.

But almost all my teammates also had a parent, sibling, or relative who'd played hockey at a high level. That's usually how young kids get started in the first place, since it's the kind of sport that tends to be passed on through the generations. So my hockey story is a bit different in that way.

MY GRANDFATHER'S NAME WAS NAZEM KADRI. He was the Original Gangster. Back in the 1960s, he and my grandmother, Sharfi, left Lebanon with their kids to escape war. His older brother had left before he did, settling in Brazil where he started a family, and my grandfather was very close to moving there to join him. But the brothers also had some relatives who'd moved to Canada, so the OG decided to head north.

It's funny how the stars align. A decision made decades ago can change the whole course of your life. My grandfather's move to Canada allowed me to become who I am. Without that move, it's unlikely that I'd ever have found my way to the ice.

My grandparents didn't know English when they settled in a small town just outside of London—the largest city in southwestern Ontario, which sits almost exactly midway between Toronto and Detroit.

My grandfather was a hardworking, blue-collar guy. It's hard to find steady employment in a new country while you're struggling to understand its language. But Nazem Kadri was a grinder. He came from a traditional background, the kind of generation where life's main pursuit was to go to work and make money for your family. So not only did he hold several factory jobs, but he also took on extra work to support his wife and their seven children.

After a long day in an automotive factory, at night he'd clean the Fleetway bowling alley, one of those large ten-pin places that would host league competitions and children's birthday parties. My grandfather would often bring my father and his brother along. My dad, Samir—known as Sam—would tell me stories about the fun they all had, with the entire alley to themselves. But it was also work. They were expected to pitch in wherever they could. Dad would help clean the place all night, doing the graveyard shift with his brother, and then go to school in the morning.

That's how the Kadri family would always operate as they built a life in Canada. We still work hard and we stick together. Today there are probably fifty or sixty of us, and most of my relatives live in the London area to this day.

I always appreciated hearing stories like that while I was growing up. My grandparents set an example for us all. It's where a lot of my work ethic comes from.

When my father first arrived in Canada, he tried to find his way as a child in a new world. Having quickly discovered how much his classmates loved hockey, he learned the game on his street alongside other kids his age. But he was never able to play the game as an organized sport; as a new Canadian, he was never given the opportunity. Extracurriculars weren't very high up on the list of priorities for those getting their start in a new country, and Samir needed to help support the family.

Yet my father was a very good athlete. And he's a competitor still—probably one of the most competitive people I know, which is saying something. He played football and basketball at Montcalm Secondary School, and was just naturally gifted at whatever sport he took on. Samir was always active, even if he wasn't playing organized sports beyond high school. Hockey was the sport he loved the most, though.

My parents met when they were young, as members of London's small Muslim community, and they married young, too. Both of their families attended the London Muslim Mosque. My mother's parents were also from Lebanon, although she was born in Canada. Not having migrated meant it was a bit of a different story for her; she was a London girl who lived in the city her whole life. Still, she was a first-generation immigrant, and her family had to work hard to get by.

Like their parents, Sam and Sue Kadri were grinders. And both were determined to give me and my sisters all the opportunities they didn't have when they were younger. My father found work in the automotive industry, just as his father had. My mother was a cashier at Loblaws. We didn't have much, but I never felt I lacked anything. My two older sisters and I knew we were lucky to have the kind of parents we did.

We bounced around a lot. When I was young, we lived in several different houses, meaning I went to a few different elementary schools. Moving was a part of life back then; we weren't in a great position financially, which likely contributed to all the relocations. At one point we stayed in a house with other relatives in our extended family. It was an epic time for me as a kid, living there with several of my cousins, all of us around the same age. I was having such a blast that I didn't really realize we were struggling. Those are some of my fondest memories, being under the same roof with as many as five other families at the same time.

IT WAS THROUGH THOSE EARLY years that my father and I bonded over hockey. It was always me and my old man. And we couldn't have been in a better place to learn the game together, since London is one of Canada's great hockey cities. There's something organic about the sport in my hometown. It's a game that most kids play and have some kind of relationship to.

I was seven or eight when we started trekking out each week to the old London Ice House, a vintage rink in the middle of nowhere, to watch the London Knights. There'd be so many cars around it that we'd usually have to park way down the country sideroad the barn sat on, with what felt like a two-mile jog to its front door. Dad would often put me on his shoulders and carry me to the gate. As soon as we walked in, we'd be hit by the enticing smell of popcorn, and after picking up a box at the concession, we'd find our place on the bleacher-style seating that wrapped around the rink. After the anthem ended, the bright overhead lights would flash on and the freshly flooded ice would shine beneath them.

Then the puck dropped. I was enthralled by everything going on around me—the people, the yelling, the chaos on the ice. I was in love with all of it.

I used to be so amazed at how these players did their line changes, hopping over the boards like it was nothing. How did they do that? It was so impressive to me. I'd watch a guy shoot the puck into the air from his own end clear to the other side of the ice on a penalty kill. How was *that* even possible? I wanted to be able to do it too, but I could barely raise the puck.

There I'd sit beside Dad, usually munching on the chocolate bar I'd convinced him to buy after the popcorn, feeling as though we were watching the best hockey players in the world.

I didn't go to any professional games growing up. It was always junior hockey. We couldn't afford to head down to Toronto and watch an NHL game. So the London Knights were our thing. That's where hockey came alive for me.

AS I GOT OLDER I'D SPEND hours playing road hockey with my buddies on the street, or outside in the backyard, or over at a friend's house. And if I wasn't playing some sort of hockey with my neighbourhood friends, I'd be at the rink. I just loved to skate. It was around this time when my parents started to realize how much I enjoyed being out there.

That's one thing I've learned in the years since. If you're trying to mould a young person into an elite player, first and foremost they have to be passionate about it. You can't pull them by the hair and try to force them to excel in a sport. All our passions and talents are unique. Kids will find them as they grow. If they're fortunate, they'll find a way to build a life doing what they love. And if they do, it's an incredible gift. That's all you can ask for as a mom or dad.

A young person has to find their own love for the game. If a kid dreads going to practice every single day—especially young kids— hockey will be ruined for them.

I loved every minute of it and was lucky that my parents did everything they could so that I could play. Then, as I got older, we started to bear down on the commitment.

I worked endlessly on the street, in the backyard, and at the rink. And I tried to emulate everything I saw at London Knights games, on *Hockey Night in Canada*, and in the endless highlights I consumed. I studied the game.

In later years, I'd admire players like Vinny Lecavalier, Pavel Datsyuk, and Joe Thornton—each a different kind of player, with unique aspects to his game that I could learn from. Joe was a local hero; I even had his poster on my wall. He's from St. Thomas, not too far from London—and he was a first overall pick in 1997 by the Boston Bruins, when I was seven years old. (A couple of decades down the road, I'd hold a chunk of old man Jumbo's beard in my fist during a fight—but we'll get to that later.)

At the time, I took a lot from each one. I'd never be able to play as well as any of them individually, but I learned from the way they played the game and made elements of each player's style my own. I'd try to notice guys' tendencies and what they did really well—and then try to add it to my repertoire. Those guys did the same with the players they admired. You end up creating something unique to yourself.

My biggest idol in those early years was Paul Kariya. At the time I always wore number 9, dreaming of being just like him. I loved the way he played the game, as any kid growing up in that era did. I don't think there's a hockey fan out there who doesn't admire Kariya. It's impossible not to. He was incredibly skilled and very competitive, but he was also a tough little guy who never backed down. And since I was small for my age all through elementary and middle school, I saw myself in him.

I also liked that Kariya looked a bit different out there. His Asian heritage made him look more like me than any other player I watched in the NHL.

For in minor hockey, it was apparent, in my young innocence, that I too was different. I remember looking around at an early age, realizing I was the only Brown guy in the dressing room. My teammates were always a bunch of white guys. At the time, though, I didn't think anything of being a minority in hockey. I always just felt I was part of the team. And my teammates were great—some of them remain my closest friends today. So when I was that age I didn't know much about my unique place in the game. I was just out there being a kid, enjoying being on the ice.

OVER THE COURSE OF MY years playing AAA in London, hockey became a central part of our lives. I had tons of support; my whole family would often come to my games. And my grandfather was always in my corner. I remember him standing right up against the glass, cheering as loudly as anyone. He even used to bribe me with chocolate bars: every time I scored, I'd get another one. I think he understood how much I enjoyed playing. It wouldn't have mattered how good I was, really; he was going to cheer me on no matter what. I don't think he really understood the magnitude of what I could do and where I could go, but he was forever rooting for me. He found joy in seeing all his grandkids pursue their passions.

From the time I was six, we travelled all over—to places like Chatham, Sudbury, Toronto, Windsor, and Detroit. Sometimes we'd drive as far away as Chicago for a tournament. We often had seven or eight travelling tournaments a year, where you'd have to stay in hotels for several days. We went as a family and would try to make the most of it: the bunch of us would hop in the car, drive for hours to the tournament, and stay in a hotel room together. And we'd always have a good time, from what I remember—although if you asked my two older sisters, you might hear a different story. Since we didn't have much help with child care, it wasn't as though we could just leave part of our family behind in London and head out of town for the weekend. So we'd all just pack a bag and away we'd go.

My sisters were good sports through it all. We had a lot of fun and spent a lot of quality time together, which was great. But at the time, I took for granted all this family travel, which was for me alone.

Now I know for a fact that they didn't want to spend their time in an ice-cold arena. They've reminded me of it many times. (I have four sisters, two older and two younger; the latter were born when I was in my late teens.)

As a kid, you don't realize how lucky you are when you're surrounded by love. I didn't understand that at all. My sisters always came out and supported me, even when they got older and weren't forced to come. They've been there when times were great and when times weren't so great. They stuck it out for me, and I'm always going to love them for it. I'm fortunate to have a family like that.

My parents never complained about the cost of my dreams, but it got pretty pricey and was a lot for them to manage. Even though they'd always try to give us everything they could, playing hockey and travelling to tournaments would put a hole in anyone's pocket. Hockey is an insanely expensive sport, and for many kids, playing rep is almost impossible to afford.

There were times when the family finances were so tight that my parents struggled to keep up with payments. My dad had to find other sources of income to make sure I could keep playing hockey. He used to play Proline—a sports betting game you'd play at a variety store, where you'd try to pick who was going to win certain games, and if you got them all correct, you'd get a payout. One day, he hit one of those. Because of that, he was able to pay for our travel and hotel for one of my tournaments away. If he hadn't won, he wasn't sure how he was going to cover the tab.

That's how it was. My dad was always just trying to do whatever he could to get me through it. Those are stories we laugh about now, but I can't imagine what it must have been like to go through that in real time. Thanks to my parents, I never had to worry about that kind of reality.

That sacrifice was part of a wonderful gift they gave me through-out my childhood: the gift of belief.

Although I was good at a young age, I was never really the best on my team growing up. But my father knew I was different and believed I had the potential to make a career out of the game we loved. Today he tells this story often: He was late the day I was born; my mother went into labour while he was still rushing to the hospital from work. As he drove, the song "Big League" by Tom Cochrane came on the radio, about a father watching his son's determination as he tries to make it to the NHL. To Dad, that was a sign of big things to come.

For me, one of the early nods to my aspirations came as I was becoming known in London as a hockey player. Some of my team-mates and classmates struggled to pronounce my name properly. They called me Naz-Zeem, elongating the E. I was used to it. People used to butcher the name Kadri all the time. But when you're a kid, friends start creating nicknames. Owing to the common mispronunciation of my name and my talent as a player, I started to be called Naz-Zeem The Dream. Aside from the fact that The Dream didn't rhyme with my actual name, I took to it. More than a nickname, it felt like a call-ing. It stuck with me as I set out to make that dream come true.

AS WE PURSUED THE SIGN that the hockey gods had given my father, he did his best to shield me from what it meant to be a minority in a white person's game. Inevitably, though, incidents would happen.

I was probably just ten or eleven when I began hearing some vulgar shit. It gets competitive out there. You understand the inten-sity of the sport and that both teams are trying to win. But when that stuff comes into play it's disheartening. What was worse was that most of it came from parents in the stands. And when you're a kid, adults know everything; their words carry weight and authority.

Racism is really hard to process when you're young. I remember feeling confused, not knowing what most of the names I was called even meant—names that were coming from grown-ass people. Fortunately, I had conversations with my parents about it. They helped me navigate through those moments and prepare for many more to come.

Even though it wasn't that long ago, it was a different era. People are held more accountable now if they behave that way in front of kids. But back then no one did anything about it. You'd have to just shake it off and away you go.

Whenever it would happen, Dad would reiterate that there are a lot of ignorant people out there. People who aren't really that educated about the world and don't know much about culture. He taught me to develop that "shake it off" mentality.

"Shut everybody up with what you do on the ice," he would tell me.

I took that to heart and played with that emotion—a fire, deep within me. I went out and shut a lot of those leagues up. They didn't have much to say after that.

But I'd face racism at every level I'd play. It never goes away. Through it all, I'd carry that lesson my father taught me. I'd be a grinder, like my grandfather. I'd be a dreamer, like my dad. And every time I'd step on the ice I'd grit my teeth and show the hateful bastards just what a Brown kid on skates is capable of.

2
GROWING OUT OF MY PROM SUIT

BEFORE MY GRADE-EIGHT PROM at Jack Chambers Public School, I got dressed up in my best suit and did what any hockey-mad thirteen-year-old would do; I went to the garage, picked up my hockey stick, and practised stickhandling a golf ball. My father walked in holding his camcorder, one of those old clunky ones you had to hold up to your eye. He wanted to document this important moment in my life. Then he asked a question that any Canadiens-loving hockey dad would ask his son before heading out to mark the end of middle school with his friends.

"Hey, what if Toronto drafts you?"

I stopped the golf ball with my blade and looked straight into his camera.

"Hell no," I said. "No way. I ain't going."

But at that time in my young career it wasn't clear that I'd be going anywhere. I was still a dreamer then, watching the NHL on television, attending Knights games, and playing hockey on the ice or on the road every chance I got.

I was skating for the London Junior Knights in the Minor Hockey Alliance of Ontario—a loop of rep teams that operates mostly in the southwestern part of the province. As I've said, I was among the more skilled players on the ice, but never the best on my team. It didn't help that I was short and skinny. Although it didn't affect my ability, I knew that my size hurt me. And as players around me started to sprout up and gain muscle, I felt like a child. If any NHL scouts saw me playing at that time, they'd probably have laughed at my ambition to make it to the show. I was a confident kid, but I was also self-aware. My dreams were a long shot. Hell, I'd probably even report to the Maple Leafs if they'd have me.

With the NHL a distant mirage, my more immediate hope was to play well enough to be noticed by scouts in the Ontario Hockey League.

To that end, I was always working, always trying to improve my craft. Even in a suit ready for prom, if there was a stick nearby, I'd be picking it up and practising. For me, hockey was all I wanted and all I needed. I was captain of most of the teams I played on and thrived in that leadership role. I'd built a reputation as one of the better players in our minor hockey system and through the league.

But no matter what I did, my size remained a problem. I could eat ten cheeseburgers and wouldn't gain a pound. (Of course, now I have the opposite problem.)

IN 2005 THE LONDON KNIGHTS hosted the Memorial Cup at the John Labatt Centre—the brand-new arena in the heart of the city's downtown that had replaced the Ice House as the Knights' home. The facility was one of the nicest in major junior hockey at the time, with seating for more than nine thousand people. It was like a tiny version of an NHL rink. Everything about it felt professional.

Back in 2000 the Knights had been bought by Dale and Mark Hunter alongside Basil McRae. Bringing their decades of NHL experience to the franchise, the trio started piecing together a dominant junior hockey roster, with several players who would go on to the NHL.

Dad and I were regulars in the Labatt Centre's fancy new seats as the Knights set an OHL record with 110 points in 2003–2004 (although they lost to the Guelph Storm in the OHL Western Conference final). The next season, as London prepared to host the Memorial Cup, the team set a Canadian Hockey League record by going thirty-one games in a row without a loss—and broke their own record with 120 points on the season. The team was led by Corey Perry, who ran away with the OHL scoring title with 130 points. Dylan Hunter, Dale's son, was second with 104. Rob Schremp was fourth in the league with 90. They made up one of the most dominant lines the OHL has ever seen. Dave Bolland and Brandon Prust added grit up front. Daniel Girardi, Marc Methot, and Dennis Wideman were part of an impenetrable defensive core.

I was fourteen years old, in my first year at A.B. Lucas Secondary School and one of nine thousand fans at each game, watching some of the best junior hockey that's ever been played. The Knights swept through the playoffs, and after beating the Ottawa 67s in the final, won the team's first ever OHL championship. I'd never experienced a rush like that, being among the fans in the building and through the streets, all of us going crazy. The moment is remembered to this day in a giant mural on the Labatt Centre facade. That team remains a legend in my hometown.

It was an addictive feeling. I wanted to be part of something like that.

When the Memorial Cup began in London a week later, the city was on fire. And for a young player, it was an absolute dream.

Sidney Crosby came to town with the Rimouski Oceanic. Shea Weber arrived with the Kelowna Rockets. And here was Corey Perry and our hometown team. I was in complete awe of how these guys played the game. But instead of being a wide-eyed kid, now I was a teenager with ambition. I knew I had the skill to reach the OHL. I knew I could skate with these guys.

I also knew that dreams become reality only when you work hard enough to pull them into view. You don't reach that level without putting everything you have into it.

It was during that summer, as I was nearing fifteen and about to enter grade ten, that I finally grew out of my prom suit. Almost overnight I was the same size as everyone else on the ice. I was stronger and faster, too. All the work I'd put into improving my ability as a playmaker—stickhandling, passing, shooting, all the fundamentals—now paid dividends. I still wasn't a huge guy by hockey standards; I was probably about a buck forty. But the added size and strength was all I needed. I was able to elevate my game and began to surpass all the guys who'd been ahead of me before.

THAT SEASON, I LIT UP the league and became one of the top players for my age group in the province. By the end of it we knew I'd be a first-round pick in the OHL draft. For the first time it seemed the mirage could turn into something tangible.

Suddenly I had multiple options to mull over. Like most kids playing at that level, I had to consider whether I'd be best suited to playing major junior hockey or pursuing an athletic scholarship to play for a Division I school in the NCAA. I contemplated which direction to go and even did a few college visits. In the end, I was pretty certain I'd go the junior route. That was the hockey I'd grown up watching with such wide eyes. It was the closest I could get to my dreams. It wasn't a difficult decision for me. But nobody else knew that at the time.

Another critical factor was that I didn't feel ready to go far from home at such an early age. My entire life to that point had been with my family. We were a unit. Playing somewhere several hours from London would be a huge leap, and I wanted to avoid it. So when I was talking with teams that were considering drafting me but were far away, I made it clear that I was seriously weighing the college route. Because I was expected to go early in the first round, these teams would be running the risk of wasting a high pick on someone who might not join the franchise at all. It's one of the unique elements of leverage a teenage player has if they're lucky enough to be in that position.

As young as I was, I knew it was important to take as much control of my future as possible. Hockey has always been a game that pushes back against that kind of autonomy. Decades ago, players would sign on with a junior team that was affiliated with a pro team—and they would remain the property of that team until it said otherwise. Bobby Orr played for the Oshawa Generals, which was an affiliate of the Boston Bruins at the time. If Orr had played for the Kitchener Rangers, he'd have become a New York Ranger, and if he'd played for the Hamilton Red Wings, he'd have joined Gordie Howe in Detroit. Today, the control players have over their futures has come a long way since the 1960s. But people in the hockey world still bristle at the idea of players using whatever means possible to determine where they want to play—especially in junior. So I make no apologies for misleading teams that were interested in me but that I had no intention of playing for.

At the 2006 OHL priority draft, I watched anxiously as each team selected—hoping my name wouldn't be called too soon. Steven Stamkos went first overall to the Sarnia Sting. Michael Del Zotto went second to the Oshawa Generals. Alex Pietrangelo went third to the Mississauga Ice Dogs. As every subsequent name was called, I felt like I'd dodged a bullet—some worse than others. The London Knights had the last pick in the first round. It would have been a dream to play for the team I grew up watching. I had a good relationship with Mark and Dale Hunter. I'd played with both of their sons in minor hockey. But I knew it was unlikely that I'd get that far. As the first round neared its end, Cody Hodgson went seventeenth to the Brampton Battalion. Finally it was the Kitchener Rangers' turn to select.

I'd met with Pete DeBoer, who was the Rangers' head coach at the time, and we'd connected right away. Pete was an accomplished OHL coach who was destined for a bigger stage. In a couple of seasons he'd become head coach of the Florida Panthers, and he's coached in the NHL ever since. Kitchener was a little more than an hour from London, which meant I'd still be close to my family. They were one of the few teams I hoped to play for.

When I heard my name called that day, I remember feeling a rush of excitement and relief: "The Kitchener Rangers select Nazem Kadri."

Hell yeah—I was on my way.

3
A SCRAWNY KID AMONG MEN

WHEN NO ONE WAS LOOKING, I grabbed as many rolls of tape as possible from a box in the locker room and stuffed them around my waistband.

I was desperate for whatever weight I could add before stepping on the scales during my physical with the Kitchener Rangers' trainers. At least I *appeared* a bit wider.

Even though I'd gone through a growth spurt, I was still a light-weight compared to the much older players in major junior. When I arrived for training camp my rookie season in 2006, my playing weight was still only 140 pounds—which was about as scrawny as it comes in the OHL, where I'd be playing against fully grown twenty-year-olds who in some cases weighed forty to fifty pounds more than I did. It was a challenge. I felt pretty insecure about it. And when the other players saw me without my gear on, I sensed them looking at me funny and thinking, "*That's* our first-round pick? He's scrawny as shit."

Despite my being at the smaller end, the Rangers told me they loved the way I played. The team believed I was still growing into my body, but even so, they were taking a bit of a gamble on how I'd develop physically and how that would translate to my effectiveness as a player.

I tried to pack on as much weight as possible, but the cheeseburgers still wouldn't stick.

My rookie season was a tough learning curve for me.

I was trying to feel out the process of playing at a higher, faster, stronger level. At just fifteen, I'd already faced so much doubt and adversity in my career. I thought of all the times I'd been told I was too small to make it in hockey, and of all the times I'd been targeted in rinks across Ontario because of the name on my jersey and the colour of my skin. Now, though, I'd arrived at my chance to tell everyone who doubted me—and especially those who hated me because of my identity—exactly where to shove it.

Even for a scrawny guy, Kitchener was a great place to play. The Rangers are owned by fans who are shareholders in the club, which creates a real sense of community around it. The city acts as a big market for an OHL team and carries a storied past. And the Kitchener Memorial Auditorium—known as the Aud—is an icon barn, a living hockey museum. It was built in the early 1950s and just has this classic aura about it. You walk into the place and know that history has unfolded there. Even though it's undergone several renovations and expansions, the Aud retains a majestic feel. It helps that Kitchener is one of the most successful teams in Canada's major junior system, with more than 180 players and coaches from the club who went on to NHL careers.

But despite playing for a great organization, the advancement to junior was a wake-up call for me. Plus, I was away from home for the first time. Adapting to both at once was difficult.

It helped that my family was only an hour and a half away. I was very grateful that I hadn't ended up on the other side of the province. My parents and sisters would come down to watch my games every weekend, creating my very own cheering section. But even with those visits, I still lived in a new environment, with a new family. Everything felt out of sorts.

There were a lot of growing pains to go through on the ice that first year in junior. It was a big leap from minor hockey, even at its highest levels, to a league where the best players from ages fifteen to twenty play alongside each other. Some of these guys were basically full-grown men. And when you're a teenager, a few years is an enormous gap. Everyone was stronger, and the pace of play was much faster. It was harder to stand out. I had to find my way. I was confident that I had the skill to compete, but I had to evolve as a player to get there.

Looking back, it's easy to see that it was a pretty normal time of transition for a young athlete. But at the time, it was deeply frustrating. I played mostly on the third and fourth line.

And here I'd been a highly touted pick who'd lit up my AAA minor midget loop. It didn't matter to me that I was the youngest player on the team. I expected better of myself. I understood that I wouldn't be the best player on the ice, but it was demoralizing to feel as if I'd taken several steps back. And yet throughout that time I was actually moving forward, learning to adapt—coming into my own as a player.

That winter, in late February 2007, I joined a stacked Team Ontario at the Canada Winter Games in Whitehorse alongside future NHLers like Steven Stamkos, Alex Pietrangelo, Adam Henrique,

Cody Hodgson, and Michael Del Zotto. I played well, and we won the gold medal. That tournament gave me a boost of confidence. But when I stepped back on the ice with the Rangers, I still felt outmatched by the strength and speed of the older players.

We finished the year with a disappointing second-round exit in the playoffs. Through sixty-two games as an OHL rookie, I'd scored just seven goals and had fifteen assists for twenty-two measly points.

THAT SUMMER I PUT IN even more work on and off the ice, determined to make a statement when I returned to Kitchener.

I was hard on myself, which I think helped push me to constantly find ways to improve. I learned that from my father.

My old man supported me and believed in me from day one, but he was always a hardass. And when I was younger, he could be pretty tough, forever holding me accountable, making sure I wasn't slacking off in games or practices. Dad set that standard. It was a high bar, and I didn't always reach it.

He also knew a lot about the game and had a great eye for what unfolded on the ice. Which was weird, given that he'd never played organized hockey himself; I'd always wondered how he'd managed to develop such a sharp sense of its nuances. But whether or not I was willing to admit it, I was astonished by my father's hockey IQ. He taught me how to play—and, once I'd figured that out, he taught me how to play well.

There were times when he'd get pissed off and probably went a little overboard, but looking back, I probably deserved it. It didn't matter whether it was a game or a practice: if I didn't try my hardest on the ice, I'd be walking home.

That happened a few times. Dad would stop the car at the side of the road and say, "Get your ass out and walk."

I was thirteen or fourteen at the time, and there I'd be, in the middle of winter, trudging along with my bag and stick over my shoulder. And it was always quite a hike home; I'd be out in the snow for a good half hour. Couples out for a stroll would pass me, probably thinking, "What the hell is this kid doing?"

At the time, I'd be mad. I thought Dad was a maniac. But now I can see that it helped forge my toughness as a player and my resilience as a person. It made me who I am today. I have a lot of fortitude; I can take a lot of heat. And I think a lot of that mental toughness comes from my dad.

He believed that I had what it took to succeed in this game, and he didn't want to see me squander an opportunity he'd never been given. This was the man who'd always find a way to buy me a new pair of hockey skates or a brand-name stick even though we didn't really have the funds. I wasn't aware of that sacrifice at the time, and I couldn't appreciate it. But I'd be pissed too if I'd worked so hard to afford these things and my son was out there half-assing it.

My father knew the cost of dreams. After a car accident that left his own father unable to work, at fourteen he knew what it was like to spend all night alongside his brother cleaning a bowling alley and then going straight from that alley to school, never letting on to their classmates. He knew there were no days off when you're trying to give your family a chance at a better future. So I can understand now why he reacted the way he did when he saw me slacking off despite my abilities. Dad was hard on me because he loved me, and because he loved our family.

My mom was the balance. If Dad was bearing down she'd jump in and cheer me up. And she was always the sunny, positive one in the stands. No matter what I did out on the ice, she was there to support me and make me feel good. I loved her so much for it. I don't know if my parents ever intended it that way, but it was a nice little combo they had going on.

I believe there was a lot of thought behind my dad's approach, though. Much of the time, I think he was testing me. He wanted to see what I was made of—and he always knew how to press my buttons. When he was tough on me there were times when I'd snap back, and we had a few verbal altercations. But a lot of the time I'd respond really well: I'd be bitter but I'd get over it. And if I'd had a bad performance I'd bounce back better and stronger. I was too competitive to stay down on myself; I was more focused on proving the doubters wrong. It's something I've always had inside of me, and I think deep down Dad knew that and felt he had to try to bring out my best.

At the end of the day, that's my old man right there. He's been my guy since day one. And that's never going to change.

So, when I went home during the off-season after my rookie year with the Rangers, I felt the fire that my father had helped me turn into fuel. I worked my damn ass off all summer. I hit the gym hard and skated whenever I could. No way was I going to have another season like my first.

WHEN I RETURNED TO KITCHENER to start my second OHL season, everything changed. It all clicked for me. I'd bulked up. I was stronger on the puck. I was faster—and the game slowed down for me. The nineteen- and twenty-year-olds I was playing against no longer had an advantage over me. I know it had as much to do with my mindset as it did with my physical ability. There's no denying that as I grew and gained muscle, I became better equipped to hold my own. But I also had more swagger and grit to my game. I was a huge Kobe Bryant fan and an early adopter of his Mamba Mentality. I knew I was in charge of how far I'd take this journey, that I'd work as hard as I could to make my dream my reality. I believed in what I could become. No one was going to get in my way.

The Kitchener Rangers were selected as hosts for the Memorial Cup that season, which meant we'd have a spot in the final tournament regardless of whether we won the OHL championship or not. But our squad didn't need the bye. Under coach Pete DeBoer we ran away with the league title, finishing the season with 110 points—28 points ahead of our London Knights rivals, who finished second in the Midwest Division. It was one of the most memorable seasons of my career. All year it felt as though we were on the brink of something great.

I was lucky to play for a guy like Pete as I found my way. Pete believed in me. He put his trust in me and helped guide me as a young player as I transitioned through that rough patch. Even when I was a third- and fourth-line player, he always encouraged me. Pete knew it was temporary, and he made sure I believed it.

That year I became one of the best young players in the league. I went from scoring seven goals in a season to being a twenty-five-goal scorer, adding forty assists for sixty-five points—averaging close to a point per game. I'd arrived.

The Rangers were in an all-or-nothing mode that season. It was apparent early on that the team was all in. Hosting the Memorial Cup was a huge deal not only for the community but for us as well. Those breaks don't come along very often. And we actually had the talent to win it. Pete was likely heading to an NHL coaching position the following year, and several players would be moving on as well. This team had one chance to make it work.

As the season continued, we stocked up on top players to ensure a good run at the Cup. Then, in January, Pete approached me with a proposition. The team was trying to put together a deal to bring in Steve Mason—one of the best goaltenders in junior—from the London Knights. Steve was in his final season; he'd been drafted by the Columbus Blue Jackets and was headed to the NHL the next year. The catch was that the Knights wanted me in return. But not right away. Instead, London was willing to trade Mason to the Rangers in exchange for two players and "future considerations." And those future considerations were me.

Pete asked if I was okay being the unspoken part of the deal. They told me they wouldn't make the trade if I wasn't.

I loved playing in Kitchener, especially that season. But I could see where this was heading. Next year would be much different for the Rangers: with Pete gone, it would be the start of a new era. And here I had a chance to return to London, live at home, and play for the team I'd grown up playing for. Plus I knew owners Dale and Mark Hunter well and had a great deal of respect for them. So although the circumstances were odd, it was also kind of a perfect situation.

I called my parents and asked what they thought. We agreed to the deal.

The deal went through; Mason joined our roster for those future considerations; we surged toward the playoffs. I spent the rest of the season knowing that I'd effectively been dealt—but that I was also going to play in the Memorial Cup. We went up against the Knights several times, which was bizarre because I knew that most of my opponents would be my teammates soon.

We plowed through the playoffs, knocking off Plymouth, Sarnia, and Sault Ste. Marie—losing just twice—before meeting the Belleville Bulls in the OHL championship. The Bulls had led the Eastern Conference all season. It was a battle of the best two teams in the province, and fittingly the series went seven games before we came out on top, hoisting the J. Ross Robertson Cup as OHL champions.

I'd continued to play well throughout the playoffs, scoring nine goals and twenty-six points in twenty games, so I felt all the more confident in facing our next challenge.

A WEEK LATER, THE BEST TEAMS in junior hockey met at the Aud to play in the Memorial Cup.

The Western Hockey League was represented by the Spokane Chiefs, while the Gatineau Olympiques, led by Claude Giroux, represented the Quebec Major Junior Hockey League. And after beating up on each other for seven games, we joined the Belleville Bulls as the best from the Ontario Hockey League—the Bulls given a spot just because we were already in the tournament as hosts.

For me, being part of the Memorial Cup was a dream. I couldn't believe I was there, playing for one of hockey's most iconic trophies, the pinnacle of what a player my age can compete for. I can't overstate how it felt. Beyond representing Canada at the World Juniors, there's nothing like it. The atmosphere was unreal, and the hockey was thrilling. We beat Gatineau 6–5 in overtime in our first game. The noise in the Aud was deafening. After that, we dropped our next round-robin game to Spokane, 2–1—and then lost to Belleville 2–1 in overtime.

But we had our final revenge over Belleville in the semifinal—our ninth game against the Bulls in under a month.

Less than a minute into the first, I one-timed a pass in the high slot that found its way through a crowd and past Mike Murphy in goal. It was the biggest goal of my life up to that moment. I roared at the crowd as they erupted. The energy in that building was like nothing I'd ever experienced before. It carried us. Matthew Halischuk scored another for us eight minutes later. Then, with seven minutes to go in the first, I took the puck at a high circle and curled back toward the blue line. As I skated I dropped the puck behind me just as Justin Azevedo cut away from a defender and fired a rocket over Murphy's glove. The surge continued. Then, a couple of minutes later, on a two-on-two break, Halischuk slipped a perfect pass to Nick Spalding, who tapped in our fourth.

The game was over. And no way were we letting the Bulls back in: we put them out of their misery in the second, adding three more goals to wipe out any lingering hope they might have had.

It ended 9–0. I couldn't believe it: we were heading to the Memorial Cup final. The Aud exploded into a giant party. For the franchise, it marked the seventh time they'd made the final, tying the Peterborough Petes as the team with the most Memorial Cup championship appearances dating back to 1972. But to Kitchener fans, reaching the final at home, after earning every step along the way, seemed the greatest moment in team history. It was incredible to be part of it all.

Sadly, we couldn't complete the storybook ending. We met Spokane in the final, and although the Chiefs didn't have our high-powered offence, they played lockdown defence, smothering our chances. We fired everything we could at goalie Dustin Tokarski, but he fended it off perfectly. We trailed 3–1 heading into the third and continued firing at him; the shots were 25–7 in our favour in the final frame alone. We just couldn't find the net.

Watching the Chiefs celebrate as the horn blew on our 4–1 defeat was the worst feeling I'd experienced in hockey. This sport can be such a damn rollercoaster.

Boos rained down on the Chiefs as they accepted the Memorial Cup on our ice. Then, as they passed the Cup around, it split apart and fell to the ice. The thing turned out to be a replica. The real one, which has been around since 1919, lives at the Hockey Hall of

Fame. I guess they don't trust a bunch of teenagers to hoist that kind of history.

We were second best. It was one of many bitter moments to come in my career. But these were the kinds of moments that help fuel that passion to win. Part of becoming a champion is knowing what it's like to lose—and hating that feeling more than anything.

I'd stepped on the ice that night in Kitchener knowing it would be my last game for an incredible organization. In just two years I'd evolved into the kind of player I believed I could be. There was still a long way to go, but now I knew without a doubt that I could make it to the NHL. I knew I belonged. Kitchener gave me that. Pete DeBoer and the Rangers' coaching staff gave me that. And my teammates— this incredible group that had become like brothers, fighting beside each other through the gruelling grind of the season and then the playoffs—had helped write the best chapter yet in my hockey story.

But it was over now. And not just until next year. We all knew that this had been our chance. We'd gone all in, and there was no coming back.

The next season, Pete DeBoer would leave to coach the Florida Panthers. The Rangers would finish ninth in the Western Conference and miss the playoffs. And I'd be back home—skating for one of Kitchener's biggest rivals—an hour and a bit down Highway 401.

I knew it all in that moment, on the ice, as the defeat sank in. It made it all that much harder to stomach. I'll never forget that feeling. It hurt like hell.

4
HOME-ICE ADVANTAGE

WHEN I STEPPED ON THE ICE as a member of the London Knights for the first time, it felt surreal. That's the only way to describe it.

I was realizing a boyhood dream while also returning to the hockey of my youth. So as I looked around the John Labatt Centre at nine thousand Knights fans, I pictured myself among them—a kid sitting next to his father, clutching a bag of popcorn and marvelling at the nearly pro players skating beneath the bright lights. That version of me would have been so hyped to know that he'd one day skate for the team his dad always took him to watch.

At the same time, it felt as if I were playing minor hockey again. The crowd was full of faces I recognized. My old man, mom, and sisters used to make the drive to every home game in Kitchener to watch me play. Now, in London, they sat in the stands alongside all my uncles, aunts, and cousins. I have a huge family. As players we'd get four tickets for each home game, but now there were a lot more ticket requests. I was forever trying to get more because so many people wanted to see me play. There were always dozens of my family members in the building, along with friends I'd known since we were children.

I was home. That's how it felt—as though I'd been away, but now I was back. Everything was familiar. It just felt right. It helped that I'd moved back in with my parents and sisters; I no longer felt like a guest in someone else's house. Everyone I needed in my life was right there beside me. I was even able to return to my old high school, A.B. Lucas on Tennent Avenue in London's north end, which I'd left after grade nine to move to Kitchener. For the first time since then, my life felt to be in balance again.

That's one of the difficult but often overlooked aspects of junior hockey. You don't get to live a regular teenage life. Not really. You often become a stranger in a new place at a young age, separated from your family for the first time. Your entire high school experience is thrown out of whack. Players spend most of their time at the rink, and when they're away from it, they're often with other teammates. They live, eat, and breathe hockey. You're surrounded by fans who want to cheer for you but will also turn on you quickly. So a lot of pressure comes with living that kind of reality.

Being back at A.B. Lucas while playing for the Knights was a full-circle moment for me. One of my favourite experiences as an athlete had been playing for Lucas back in grade nine. That first year of high school, playing alongside my friends, was the most normal year of my adolescence. I'd contemplated whether I should even join high school hockey, since I was trying to play at a higher level and worrying about suffering an injury on the ice. But I'm glad I made that decision: it was an incredible time and some of the most enjoyable hockey I've ever known.

There was a unique atmosphere around the team—it had a kind of college-type feel. Our coach, who was also my sports science teacher, was amazing; I still speak with him to this day. He always treated me really well and had a lot of belief in me, knowing I'd be a pretty good player. We were a great team, too, winning the high school hockey league and going on to the provincials. I was also on the high school basketball team that year.

But just like that, it was done. In grade ten I was off to Kitchener. I was grateful to have had at least one year of playing sports just for the love of it.

I still loved the game, of course, but a lot more was at stake now. My sophomore year with the Rangers had set me up as one of the top prospects in the league, and playing in the Memorial Cup had further upped the buzz around my potential. So now, playing in London in my third year, there was no escaping the expectation of the looming NHL draft that June.

We went up against Kitchener for the first time in mid-October, in front of nearly nine thousand fans at the John Labatt Centre. I was hyped for the game. The Rangers were on a six-game winning streak at the time.

There's something about playing against a team you have history with. There's a mutual respect—you're part of the team's past, after all. But as much as you still like the players and fans, you also really want to stick it to them. I had no animosity toward the organization; it's just a competitive thing. The closer you are to your opponents, the more motivation you have to make sure you win. There's an extra rush that comes with that kind of reunion matchup.

I traded chirps with several of my old teammates throughout the game, in good fun. The squad had a few quality mouthpieces, but I gave it right back to them. Then, late in the third period, I had my final say when I rushed into the Rangers' zone, going one-on-one with defenceman Myles Barbieri. I cut to the inside and then spun to the outside as Barbieri tried to close in on me; after that I left him behind and scored on goalie Parker Van Buskirk to put the game away 3–1. Having ended with a goal and two assists, it felt extra sweet to have been in on all our offence. It would be another couple of months before I'd make my return to the Aud in January. I already had the date circled in my calendar.

In London I played on a line with Akim Aliu and Jason Wilson. We clicked right away, and I led the team in scoring through our first handful of games.

But then, in mid-November, I suffered a broken jaw. It was supposed to keep me out until after the Christmas break. My jaw had to be wired shut, and I couldn't eat any solid foods—instead I drank milkshakes, protein shakes, and puréed meals of roast beef, mashed potatoes, and gravy. It was actually a lot better tasting than it sounds.

A few weeks after the injury, while still drinking my meals, I attended the World Junior selection camp in Ottawa. By that time I'd missed eight games for the Knights. I'd also lost ten pounds but was hoping to have the wires taken out soon so that I could start eating solid food again. I wasn't used to keeping my mouth closed. It was an uncomfortable feeling—almost claustrophobic. I was on the ice every day, but it was difficult to breathe when I skated.

So even though I was considered a lock as a first-round pick in the upcoming draft, the injury put me in a tough position to crack the World Junior roster, which legendary coach Pat Quinn would be selecting. It still wasn't clear when I'd be okay to play, and the tournament would begin in a few weeks, right after Christmas.

I felt I'd played as well as I could in camp, despite the injury. But I was much weaker than I'd hoped to be and felt gassed as I struggled to breathe through the wires. It was beyond frustrating: all was in jeopardy, just because of my broken jaw. And like any young player growing up in Canada, it had been one of my dreams to represent the country at the World Juniors.

The call in my hotel room came at five-forty-five in the morning. I'd been awake for quite a while, nervously waiting for the phone to ring.

It was Quinn. In his deep, distinctive voice, he told me that I hadn't made the squad. It was devastating. I'd known that all the factors were against me, but that was no consolation. I was one of the best young players in Canada and I'd wanted to represent my country against the world. Of course I understood why I hadn't been selected: I wasn't at my best and there were legitimate concerns about whether I'd be able to play. It stung, though. I'd never been cut from a team in my life.

You don't forget those moments. When you're trying to become the best player you can be, they're just as important as the moments of success.

So instead of staying in Ottawa for the World Juniors, I went back to London with something to prove. Because I was only eighteen, I'd still have one more year of eligibility for the tournament. And I was determined to prove I belonged there.

THE KNIGHTS WANTED ME TO take the rest of December off—to rest up over the holidays and put on some of the weight I'd lost.

I had no interest in that plan. Instead I returned to the team on December 19, two days after I'd been cut from the World Junior roster. As soon as I unpacked my bag in the Knights' locker room, I knew I was ready. A couple of days after that, I joined the team on the road to Peterborough to play the Petes.

I wore a cage to cover my still healing jaw.

I enjoyed playing with Aliu, another player who'd faced adversity and racism through his young career—an experience that would further align us years later, when we'd start the Hockey Diversity Alliance. He was a skilled power forward who played with a chip on his shoulder, just as I did. Aliu had made national headlines as a rookie with the Windsor Spitfire when he defended himself against hazing and ended up getting cross-checked in the face by Steve Downie (who I ended up playing with in Kitchener). Now Aliu was a Chicago Blackhawks draft pick, working to prepare himself for the NHL. We had great chemistry. I remember setting up both Aliu and my linemate Jason Wilson for goals in our 8–1 win over the Petes. That was the last time we'd play together.

Over the next two games, as I wore protective braces on my lower teeth, my face was first smashed into the glass against the Saginaw Spirit and then high-sticked against the Sarnia Sting. Later in that game Matt Martin, Sarnia's captain, hammered me with a shoulder to the chin.

"I feel fine," I lied to the *London Free Press* afterward.

With the NHL draft coming up, I couldn't afford to take any more time off. I was to be on the ice regardless of whether my jaw worked or not.

Aliu was traded to the Sudbury Wolves in early January. The next week, the Knights landed John Tavares and Michael Del Zotto from

Oshawa in a blockbuster trade involving several pieces. Tavares had just been named the World Junior MVP after leading Canada to gold in Ottawa. Since being granted exceptional status to join the OHL as a fifteen-year-old, Tavares had lived up to the hype in Oshawa, becoming the Generals' all-time leading scorer. He was widely expected to go first overall in the upcoming NHL draft. It was an all-in move that immediately put us in the Memorial Cup conversation.

Dale Hunter put John and me on a line together, moving me to the wing while John played centre. I didn't mind moving to the outside if it meant being alongside a player of his calibre. I did, however, keep my number. John and I both wore 91, but he wasn't the kind of guy to make a thing out of it. I'd switched my number from 19 to 91 when I joined London and was feeling pretty good with it. John's an absolute team player, and even though he was going to be the top pick in the NHL, he was never one to big-time his teammates. He switched to 61 without even asking about 91.

I regained my form through January, scoring twenty-eight points in fifteen games since I'd returned from my broken jaw. And John and I had chemistry on the ice right away. In our first game together I set him up to score the game winner, and we kept rolling from there. We became roommates on the road.

After writing a gruelling science exam, I hopped in the car for a game against Kitchener at the end of the month. It was a special day for me—going back to the rink where we'd accomplished so much and nearly won the Memorial Cup. At the time, the trade that had brought Steve Mason to Kitchener, while allowing me to remain there before heading to London, was still a controversial topic. The London move had been an open secret, and so it was a bit of a sideshow as I tried to focus on the playoffs with Kitchener. (After that season the OHL instituted a new rule—which most people called the

Kadri rule—preventing teams from being able to make the kind of deal that London and Kitchener had.)

I was hyped up before the return. The Aud was packed with more than six thousand people—the same great fans as ever. Still, it felt weird skating around the ice during warmups. I'd come to the organization as a fifteen-year-old kid and a lot had happened in the three years since, much of it owing to the Rangers. That building would always mean something special to me.

In some ways it felt like little had changed. But the Rangers were a shell of what we'd been. I scored early in the game on a bit of a fluky bounce off a defenceman while we were shorthanded. Then I set up John for three goals. He finished with four. I finished with four points. We crushed the Rangers 9–0.

WE SURGED THROUGH THE SECOND half of the season, finishing with nine straight wins and sitting second in the Western Conference, behind the Windsor Spitfires, heading into the playoffs. I led the Knights with twenty-five goals and fifty-three assists for seventy-eight points. It was particularly satisfying because I'd missed so many games with my broken jaw, playing in only fifty-six.

After walking through Erie and Saginaw in the first two rounds of the playoffs, it looked like we were in line for a run at the league championship. The Knights were flying. Including our streak to end the season, we had just one loss in nineteen games.

In the Conference finals we met Windsor, the top team in the league, with players like Taylor Hall and Adam Henrique. They were also one of the toughest. And Windsor was our biggest rival. It was going to be a bloody matchup.

I was playing some of my best hockey, winning hard battles and taking control of the play. It was the kind of hockey I excelled at, outworking opponents at both ends of the ice, finding ways to keep our team in games. Yet I'd dropped in the Central Scouting rankings, and the NHL draft was just a couple of months away. Earlier in the season the slight might have gotten to me. But I was playing with confidence. I was so close to hearing my name called on stage by an NHL team that I wasn't going to let a ranking bother me now.

Our series against Windsor was one of the wildest playoff match-ups in OHL history. Every single game was decided in overtime. We lost the first away, won the second at home, then battled through the next three, nearly finding a way to win each one—but failing each time. Windsor won three straight in overtime to take the series 4–1, ending our Memorial Cup hopes.

It was a bitter way to go out, knowing how close we'd been in each game—that it could have easily been a 4–1 series win. The final result couldn't capture just how close it was.

I DIDN'T HAVE MUCH TIME to dwell on the defeat, though. With the season finished, my attention turned to the NHL draft. There was a combine and all its interviews with NHL teams interested in drafting me. It felt as if I were in the middle of a two-month-long series of job interviews as I waited to learn which team would call my name.

As the date neared, I still wasn't sure where I'd land. All I knew was that we were heading to Montreal to find out, with dozens of my family members in tow.

And the very first time my father would stand in the Bell Centre, the home of his beloved Habs, would be the day he heard his son's name selected in the NHL draft.

5
THREE GENERATIONS IN MONTREAL

SEVERAL DOZEN OF MY FAMILY members had to sit in the Bell Centre's upper level. That was the only area where we were able to land seats for such a massive group at the 2009 NHL draft. It was by far the biggest section of supporters for any individual player there. And they'd all driven more than seven hours down the 401 from London to Montreal just for me.

Still, that day was about much more than me.

I'd be the one on stage, shaking hands and posing for photos. I'd be the one doing interviews and having profiles written about me for the local paper of whichever team decided to draft me. One day soon, I'd be the one skating in the NHL with the name Kadri on the back of my jersey.

But that day was about an entire family. It belonged to three generations, if not more. And as a milestone in our collective journey, it was particularly special for me that my grandfather Nazem was there to experience it. He sat in the row next to mine, along with my parents, sisters, other grandparents, and a couple of my uncles.

When the original Nazem Kadri first arrived in Canada, he didn't know anything about hockey. He just wanted to bring his family to a safe place and worked endlessly to make that possible. And now, in a massive arena filled with more than twenty thousand people, he waited to hear his grandson's name called, to witness that grandson become the highest-drafted Muslim player in NHL history. It was a dream the Original Gangster couldn't have imagined when he arrived decades before, but one that wouldn't have been possible without him.

My entire family—my parents, sisters, uncles, aunts, and cousins—all of them owned a piece of this moment. This was a family that supported each other through so many difficult days, holding together regardless of the storms we faced. We held strong.

So, one of us being drafted to the NHL? That belonged to all of us.

I sat in a section with other prospects, knowing the relentless work that each of them had put into arriving at this moment. We were all similar in that. My story was different, though, which was why an entire section of Arab people were cheering as loudly for their family as any fan in the building had ever cheered for the Habs. This was about much more than hockey.

As a top prospect heading into the NHL draft, you have a pretty good sense of where you're going. The rankings are discussed all season as Central Scouting finalizes its projected list and the media pontificate on who will wind up where. All year John Tavares was expected to go first overall, with occasional arguments that it could be Swedish defenceman Victor Hedman. Both were pretty much locks for the first two picks.

After those two future NHL All Stars, it was more of a toss-up. That year, in 2009, the draft included many players who would go on to have long NHL careers—men like Evander Kane, Matt Duchene, Brayden Schenn, Oliver Ekman-Larsson, Ryan Ellis, Zack Kassian, Nick Leddy, Chris Kreider, and Kyle Palmieri. Of course, one of the best things about the NHL is that many players who aren't selected in the first round also end up having successful NHL careers. In 2009, Ryan O'Reilly and Jakob Silfverberg were both second rounders who went on to become All Stars. Future All Star goalie Darcy Kuemper was picked a hundred and sixty-first.

I did interviews with close to thirty teams during the NHL combine, which was basically a bunch of hockey guys trying to get in your head with a bunch of silly questions. One team asked who I'd most like to have dinner with: Barack Obama, Sean Avery, or Anna Kournikova. I was an eighteen-year-old guy; what the hell did they think the answer would be? I wasn't going to bullshit.

"Anna," I answered correctly.

I was asked who I'd want to be if I could come back as anyone else.

"The greatest," I said. "Muhammad Ali."

When it came to my faith and culture, the only question I was asked was about whether I'd have to fast. I told them it wouldn't be a problem.

I knew going in that I'd likely be a top-ten pick—probably falling somewhere between five and ten. That had pretty much been the consensus all year, outside of a few haters in the media who'd probably never seen me play. We could narrow down which teams had a legitimate interest in taking me, but when you're at the mercy of a selection process, there are no certainties. Tavares went first to the New York

Islanders, which was no surprise. Hedman went to the Tampa Bay Lightning, as expected. I had a feeling that the Los Angeles Kings were thinking of taking me with the fifth overall pick, because I'd had several meetings with them, and they seemed to have shown the most interest. And I knew the Ottawa Senators needed a centre, too.

Matt Duchene went to the Colorado Avalanche third overall, and Evander Kane was selected by the Atlanta Thrashers fourth.

When the Kings stepped up to the stage next, I felt my heart pound a little faster, knowing I was in the mix. It's nerve-racking when you're waiting for your name to be called in what is the most important moment of your life, with an outcome that will dictate where you'll spend the next several years at least.

The Kings selected Brayden Schenn. I took a deep breath. I could land anywhere now. Phoenix had the next pick. After that would be Toronto, Dallas, Ottawa, and Edmonton to round out the top then. I was certain I wouldn't make it past Ottawa.

The Coyotes called defenceman Oliver Ekman-Larsson at six. Then Brian Burke, president and general manager of the Maple Leafs, walked on stage as jeers rose throughout the sold-out Bell Centre. Booing the Toronto Maple Leafs was one of Canadiens fans favourite pastimes. I knew the satisfaction of hating on the Buds well. As my father sat in the row beside me, I'm sure he felt an instinct to join the chorus.

Burke looked down at the page he'd placed on the dais and then leaned into the microphone.

"The Toronto Maple Leafs . . ." he began—the boos rose to a crescendo.

He looked up at the crowd and grinned. Then he paused for a good fifteen seconds, letting the crowd have their say. Burkie always had a sense for dramatic effect. A lone Maple Leafs fan stood proudly in his blue and white jersey waving a flag with the Leafs' logo on it. Burke continued: ". . . are pleased to select, from the London Knights of the Ontario Hockey League, Nazem Kadri."

What a feeling. An absolute rush—a dream coming true. I stood up and immediately wrapped my arms around my father, who wore a black polo with the collar popped. He hugged me hard, with all the love in him. My mother embraced me next, and with the smile of the proudest mom on the planet, she patted me on the back as she pulled me close, as though I were still her little boy.

As I pulled off my suit jacket, about to walk up to the stage and put on the Leafs' jersey, I heard the crowd booing even louder. It was incredible. Not all that long ago, if I were part of that crowd, I'd have been booing too. I love that kind of passion. But that grade-eight version of me had been a little short-sighted. I now belonged to the Toronto Maple Leafs. Would I go? Hell yes, I would.

As I reached the stairs at the end of our row, I looked up at the section filled with my family, on their feet now and cheering loudly enough to be heard over all the Habs fans. That's how we do things. No way would my clan be quiet in a moment like this. The sound of that massive collection of relatives cheering as loudly as an entire rink of fans was just perfect. Those fans had a lot of spirit, but my family had more.

Moments after my selection was announced, TSN broadcast a soundbite of Burke speaking to Bryan Murray, the general manager of the Senators, between the draft tables that had been set up on the rink. Their exchange had taken place moments before the announcement.

"What are you going to do?" Burke asked Murray.

"Well," Murray said, "I'll flip you—"

Burke interrupted him. "Kadri is the kid we're going to take." He put his hands on his hips. "Is that the kid you want?"

Murray appeared a little stunned. "Yeah."

"Okay, well we're going to take him," Burke said again.

Murray replied with a sheepish "Okay," then walked back to the Senators table.

It was another classic Burkie move. He turned to the Leafs' table. "Okay," he said. "Let's go."

That clip was all over the place after the draft, a bit of fuel added to the already heated rivalry between the Leafs and the Senators. It was a funny way for me to be thrust into the middle of it.

6
LEARNING TO CELLY

I PLAYED MY FIRST GAME as a Maple Leaf at home in London against the Philadelphia Flyers before a sold-out crowd, including all my friends and family. It was surreal, kind of like an odd dream where two places in your mind collide. There I was, playing for the Leafs but on the rink where I'd once played junior.

I scored my first goal in the blue-and-white during the first period—snapping in a drop pass from Niklas Hagman from the right faceoff dot—and celebrated as though it were the biggest goal of my career. It certainly felt that way. I was so excited that I swooped down on one knee and swept the ice. The fans went wild, too. This wasn't just a tap in on an empty net, either; I'd ended up dancing around one of their veteran defencemen. It was a highlight-reel goal—and to do it in front of everyone I loved in the city that raised me? Hell yeah, I was fired up.

When I got back to the bench, some of the older guys on the team started giving it to me for going overboard with the celly: I was just a kid who didn't understand how things went. I didn't care. Looking back on it now, though, I get it. It was a pre-season game—it didn't mean shit—but when I scored that goal I felt like the man. It was a big deal for an eighteen-year-old playing his first NHL game, representing the Maple Leafs in his hometown. I don't think they understood the magnitude of what was going through my mind (which was something like *What the fuck, this is amazing!*).

I scored again in the shootout and celebrated just as hard. Afterward Jeff Carter—another London guy, but much older than me—scored on a sweet shootout goal for the Flyers. He barely even smiled: just another day at the office for a veteran guy who'd scored a few goals before. As Carter skated by our bench he chirped me, and although I can't remember exactly what he said, it was an "act like you've been there before" kind of thing.

The thing is, Jeff, I *hadn't* been there before. That's kind of the point. I didn't know him very well but I'd looked up to him, so I'll admit I felt a bit chastised. It was a lesson learned. We've become friends in the years since, and we often joke about the day he put me in my place.

I understand how some people might have been a little choked about that one. And now, if I saw a kid sweep the ice in a pre-season game as I did, I'd probably be the one saying "What the fuck are you doing?" Still, it was one of those times when things just somehow come together. I stand by my reaction.

After the game I was named second star, and skated back out onto the ice to a massive ovation. This time I simply clapped my gloves back to the crowd. It was a wonderful moment to share with everyone who'd helped bring me to that point in my career.

IT'S SO EASY TO FORGET how young players are when they arrive at their first NHL training camp. I remember looking around the Leafs' dressing room as an eighteen-year-old thinking these were grown men, with families. Established pros. Veteran players I'd been watching in the NHL for years.

That first camp in September 2009 was a bit of a wake-up call for me. I tried to carry myself in a confident manner, but I was nervous.

Despite the nerves, it was a good camp. Rookies played a lot during the pre-season games back then. We had nine on the roster that year, but I played in every single exhibition matchup, so I had tons of chances to show what I was capable of. I held my own throughout training camp and led the whole team in points through the pre-season.

I'd come in determined to make the big club, and did everything in my power to realize that goal. But the feeling was that I'd be a long shot that season. My weight was still a concern. I had the height now, but I still had to bulk up and get committed to my off-ice routine. I was officially listed at a generous 185 pounds, but a more realistic count would have shaved a few pounds off that total.

It didn't help that Ramadan—which follows the Islamic calendar, based as it is on the lunar cycle—took place right through much of training camp, starting on August 21 that year. I had permission from my Imam to forgo a fast on each day of the month-long religious observance, because it would have been such a strain on my ability to play. But I did fast on days when I wasn't on the ice, so I certainly wasn't bulking up over those four weeks.

Despite outplaying expectations, at the end of camp, I was told that the Leafs were sending me back to junior for another year.

Burke said he felt I was ready to play in the NHL, but that I'd be worn down by Christmas. It was a good point. I knew he liked to be patient with his prospects and that he had my best interests in mind. Yet it was still so disappointing. I felt that I'd proven I could play at the next level. Nowadays if a young guy has that kind of pre-season, he's put into a role with the team right away and given every shot at success. Back then, though, in 2009, management felt it would be better to let me mature and develop more. *Develop*: that word was used a lot.

But that was the team's decision. This was in a weird period, a bit of a transition phase, when there was a lot of discussion about whether to put young guys in right away or leave them in the American League to try to develop them for the NHL, playing more minutes and all that bullshit. So it was a bit tricky for me to navigate. Although I was proud of myself, I couldn't shake the frustration.

After I was sent back to junior, Don Cherry ripped into the decision to hold me back during a *Coach's Corner* intermission segment. He set up a clip by saying he was going to show one of Toronto's best scorers, and then played a slick goal I'd scored the night before during a game with the Knights against the Plymouth Whalers. It was a nice confidence boost from Grapes.

If there was any consolation, I was happy to return to my hometown, and taking one more run with London made it easier. I had a ton of fun. But things were a bit different now that I'd generated some buzz during training camp with Toronto; a lot of talk began in the media about my potential and what I could bring to the team. And with the attention, I became more of a well-known name among Leafs fans.

It was a cool feeling for a young guy, and exactly what I'd wanted—to get my name on the map and eventually establish myself as someone hockey fans knew.

But it came with a lot of difficulties, too, because people started to recognize me. As a kid, you don't really know that people are watching you go about your business. You don't know how to watch for that kind of thing. I was naive and still had some lessons to learn about how to carry myself. A lot of it was the stuff you pick up as you go through your early years in the NHL and begin to understand what you've got to work on and how you've got to approach certain situations.

THAT YEAR, I MADE SURE there were no questions about whether I belonged on the World Junior team. And by the time I was invited to selection camp that December, I was favoured to make the squad. It helped that my jaw wasn't wired shut.

We went to the World Junior tournament in Saskatoon and Regina looking to win Canada's sixth straight gold medal. Our chances seemed pretty good. We were as stacked as Canada usually is, with players like Taylor Hall, Brayden Schenn, and Adam Henrique. I played alongside Jordan Eberle, who led the CHL in scoring at the time. Our goalies were Jake Allen and Martin Jones.

In our first game we beat Latvia 16–0, which generated a lot of debate about the tournament format and the need for a mercy rule.

I played well during the tournament, but also let my temper get out of hand a few times, which ended up becoming a media story for the wrong reasons. During our preliminary-round game against Switzerland, I got into it with one of the Swiss players. Every team comes out hard against Canada, but one guy took the chirping too far, and came at me with some racist garbage. A bit of a scrum broke out, lines were crossed, and the temperature was a lot higher for the rest of the game. Later, I skated by the Swiss bench and made a throat-slashing gesture as my way of showing I wasn't going to let that kind of thing go.

Willie Desjardins, our coach, wasn't impressed by that, and after the game he let reporters know it.

We ended up meeting Switzerland again in the semis. It was a heated contest, but it ended as a lopsided 6–1 win for us. We were on our way to play in the World Junior gold medal game, a dream I'd carried since I was young. But instead of focusing on that, I was still heated after hearing that trash on the ice. So, as we moved through the handshake line, I made a snap decision not to extend my hand to one of the guys who had made things too personal. I didn't think much of it; the omission was just a final "fuck you" from me.

But I immediately regretted it when I got off the ice. The broadcast had caught it, and the media was all over me to find out why I'd snubbed him. There was a lot of buzz, but I didn't intend to create a distraction, especially as we turned our attention to a very talented American squad. It was an important reminder to keep conflict on the ice and to not let opponents get under my skin.

THE GOLD MEDAL GAME AGAINST the United States was one of the most thrilling tugs-of-war I'd ever been part of. I've never felt so hyped up to play. The Credit Union Centre—now the SaskTel Centre—was at the peak of its fifteen-thousand-person capacity. The energy in the building was unreal, rivalling the hype I'd felt with the Rangers during the Memorial Cup.

The game went back and forth, as any good Canada–United States battle does.

We scored—they scored. They scored—we scored. They scored—we scored. It was 3–3 heading into the third period. But the Americans scored two goals early in the final frame to completely demoralize the Saskatoon crowd. With thirteen minutes left, the U.S. had a 5–3 lead.

We fought like hell to get back into it. The rest of the game was wild. I had a chance to score after Jack Campbell lost the puck behind the net, but my shot on the empty net was stopped by defenceman

John Ramage. We had several more chances as we desperately tried to stay in the game, time ticking away.

With less than three minutes to go, on the power play, Alex Pietrangelo found Eberle in the slot, who one-timed it past Jack Campbell. We were alive. I'd never felt a rush of adrenalin like that.

Time kept moving against us. Then, with under two minutes left, I fired a loose puck that hit a leg in front of the net. The puck bounced to Taylor Hall in the corner. I cut back to the boards and Hall slipped me the puck. He crossed in front of me as I backed toward the corner, then fired a pass to Ryan Ellis high in the slot on the far side. Ellis fired a shot on Campbell. The rebound bounced right to Eberle.

The rest was a blur. The puck hit the back of the net and Saskatoon erupted. We piled on Eberle in the corner. It was unbelievable—tie game, 5–5—a storybook comeback for the World Junior history books.

But the story wasn't over yet. We went into sudden death overtime, with Canada's sixth straight gold medal on the line. Both sides had chances to win it early. Those first few minutes were a pure rush. Just over four minutes in, I rushed with the puck from our end into the American zone on the right side and saw Pietrangelo pinching into the high slot looking for a one-timer. As I hit the hash marks, I dropped the puck back. Pietrangelo stepped into a rocket, firing the puck into Campbell's pads. The rebound kicked out to the hash marks on the other side, and the Americans rushed the other way on a three-on-one as I rushed back to help. Just as I reached the open man on the right side, John Carlson—my former London Knights teammate—fired a shot that beat Martin Jones on the short side.

The Americans mobbed each other on the ice. All we could do was watch, stunned. It was a brutal feeling. We'd been so close. But despite the disappointment in the 6–5 loss, there was still a sense of accomplishment among the Canadian players and from the fans cheering for us in the stands. The game had been thrilling—one of the most memorable gold medal matchups in the tournament's history. And instead of giving up when it looked like the Americans had it, we'd clawed back into the game the Canadian way. Overtime is an exciting, end-to-end coin flip.

Just being in that tournament, representing Canada, was a dream come true for me. Winning gold would have made it perfect, but we couldn't hang our heads.

I RETURNED TO LONDON FEELING good about how I'd played. Arriving on the international stage like that is a big deal in Canada, where so many fans watch the World Juniors religiously; it's a collective pastime for any Canadian kid who's grown up loving the game. Plus, playing for Canada has a huge impact on a player's profile across the league. So for me, being the Leafs' top prospect and playing for the nation at the World Juniors turned up the spotlight significantly.

And I was determined to excel in it. With less than half the OHL season left, I wanted to take the Knights far into the playoffs one last time. In other words, I wanted to make sure there was no doubt in anyone's mind that I was ready for my chance in the NHL.

I just didn't expect it to come at ten on a Monday morning in February.

7
"GAME ON"

WHEN I FIRST ANSWERED THE phone, I thought it was a joke. But it was Burke. It's very difficult to imitate that man's voice. This was real.

The Leafs had been hit by several injuries and ailments. Plus, forwards Christian Hanson and Fredrik Sjöström both had food poisoning. That left the team shorthanded that night against the San Jose Sharks, one of the best teams in the league. Meanwhile the Toronto Marlies, the Leafs' minor league team, were away on a road trip in Abbotsford, B.C.

By that time I had twenty-six goals and sixty-six points in forty-two games with the Knights—and the Leafs had been paying attention. Now they wanted me to sign a one-game amateur tryout agreement to fill a roster hole. I called my father right away and told him he'd better clear his schedule: he needed to be in Toronto that night to watch me play my first NHL game.

The team sent a car to pick me up in London and drive me to Toronto. I wasn't even part of the morning skate. Throughout that drive down Highway 401 I could feel my heart pounding; I was more nervous than I'd ever been. It didn't feel real. And as the Toronto sky-line came into view I felt the same rush I always had as a kid whenever we'd visited the city. The wall of buildings stretched into the sky, sur-rounding the CN Tower, which always seemed to pierce the clouds. Every time we made that trip it had felt like a momentous occasion.

We pulled up to the Air Canada Centre on Bay Street like I was a kid being dropped off for an AAA game. Bobby Hastings, the Leafs' assistant equipment manager, was waiting for me at Gate 2, where fans enter the building. I hopped out and strode to the trunk to grab my London Knights bag. Bobby stopped me.

"No, no," he said. "You don't carry this. Don't touch a thing. Just go get ready for the game."

He picked up the bag and threw it over his shoulder. I didn't have to carry my own bag? That's when I first felt like I was about to play in the NHL.

I walked through the Gate 2 entrance, down some stairs, across the Platinum Club lobby, then down a hallway lined with photos of the Leafs' storied history. Finally I passed through the doors of the Maple Leafs' dressing room. It was an odd feeling. I'd met most of the boys during training camp, but I didn't know any of them very well. And anyway, this was much different. I wasn't aware of anyone who'd just walked into an NHL game, mid-season, from a junior team.

I looked around the locker room and saw guys like Phil Kessel, Dion Phaneuf, Tomáš Kaberle, and Jason Blake. Here I was, a nineteen-year-old kid, in a locker room with NHL stars.

I spotted my jersey hanging in a stall: Kadri, 43. It was the number I'd been handed when I first arrived at rookie camp. Things had gone well enough, so I'd seen no need to change it up. And now there it was, hanging in the Leafs' locker room. Unreal. I would have been beaming if I wasn't so anxious.

I was quiet in the dressing room that day, having decided to mind my own business and not disrupt the order of the things. I was also just trying to focus on not embarrassing myself on the ice.

The nerves continued to build as we got closer to the game. As we stepped onto the ice for warmups, I looked around the Air Canada Centre at fans streaming into their seats. I tried to soak it in. The place was massive—and magnified in that moment.

"Holy shit," I thought. "I was playing for the Knights yesterday and today I'm playing for the Leafs. How did I get here?"

My parents had driven in from London, which meant a lot to me. After everything we'd been through, they had to be there for my first NHL game.

I looped around our end of the ice, stretching and shooting pucks, doing whatever I could not to stand out or appear as mesmerized as I was.

Act like you've been here before.

The thing is, Nazem, you haven't.

Get a grip.

The warmup flew by. By now the arena was nearly full. As the Zamboni flooded the ice I sat in my stall, my brain turning and turning. I was even more nervous than I'd been in the car on the way to the game. I was still waiting for the adrenalin to wash away the jitters.

Ron Wilson, the Leafs' head coach, came in for our pre-game pep talk and read out the starting five.

He said my name. I looked up, a little stunned. The guys gave a low cheer, hyping me up. Not only was I about to play in my first NHL game; I was also about to take the opening faceoff.

A few minutes later I stood on the blue line shuffling my skates back and forth in the dark as I listened to the Canadian national anthem. I was about to begin my first NHL game in Toronto. The fans roared as the anthem ended. Then the lights came up. Twenty thousand fans were watching me. I circled and took a deep breath.

I moved toward centre ice, where Joe Thornton lined up against me. The local legend whose poster was still on my bedroom wall at my parents' house. *Holy shit*. The Sharks were stacked. Their entire line could have been found in those collectible All-Star cards from McDonald's. Jumbo's wingers were Patrick Marleau and Dany Heatley. Dan Boyle and Marc-Édouard Vlasic were on the point. It could have been a line for the Canadian national team. Evgeni Nabokov, Russia's best tender, was in net. There were at least a few surefire Hall of Famers on the ice.

And then there was me—nineteen-year-old, undersized, still developing me.

I lined up at centre waiting for the puck to drop. Joe might have congratulated me on my first NHL game, but I don't remember anything. I was running on nerves and adrenalin. Then, when the ref dropped the puck, Jumbo whacked my stick practically into the third row and then snapped the puck back so hard it could have gone in his own net.

Holy shit, I thought again as my NHL career officially began. *Okay. Game on.*

I LAY AWAKE, STARING AT the ceiling, unable to sleep. The Leafs had put my family up in a hotel the night of my first game, but I might as well have stayed at the arena. I was way too fired up to get any rest. Excess adrenalin from the game surged through me as I replayed each moment over and over in my head, searing them into my memory. What a surreal experience.

Just like my first exhibition game, playing in front of Toronto fans in my first regular-season game seemed like a dream. I knew it was real, but I couldn't process it. Taking the opening faceoff against Jumbo? How was that even possible? And Rob Blake, twenty years older than me and an absolute legend, had been there on the ice and even wished me good luck during the game.

It was such a unique situation and it had all happened so fast. At first I'd been in awe, but after my first couple of shifts, everything settled down.

Then it was just hockey. The best hockey in the world, but hockey all the same. I knew how to play. I was confident in myself. So I just went with the flow and gave it my all, trying to do the best I could.

Later in my career, Thornton and I would get into it quite a few times. He's a competitor. But in that first game I stayed the hell away from him. I wasn't there to agitate anyone. I was just there to prove that I could be.

And as far as games go, it wasn't likely to be remembered in Maple Leafs lore. We lost 3–2. I had no shots on goal, two giveaways, and lost eleven of the thirteen faceoffs I took. But in the seventeen minutes I spent on the ice, I didn't embarrass myself.

That was the most important part: I'd shown everyone that I could skate in the show. I settled in and played my game. The players were faster and stronger than they were in junior, but it wasn't a crazy shock for me. I belonged.

Dion Phaneuf, soon to be named the Leafs' captain, kept me in check. After the game he told me to make sure I returned to the next training camp looking a little more like a man and less like a boy.

Ron Wilson, the Leafs' coach, was also quick to keep my expectations in check—setting the stage for the years to come. "He had a lot of turnovers and things he can probably get away with in junior hockey that he can't get away with in our league, let alone against a top team in the league," he told a scrum of reporters after the game.

He said it was a good opportunity for me to see what the NHL was all about.

Yeah, I'd seen what it was all about. And I knew I was ready.

BUT MY ONE-DAY CONTRACT HAD expired and I was heading back to junior. I'd known it would be one and done. So in the morning I packed up my things, grabbed my Knights gear, carried it to my parents' car, and tossed it in the trunk. We drove back to London together. (The chauffeur had been a one-way situation.)

I didn't mind. I rode that high all the way home and it stayed with me for the rest of the season. Arriving back with the Knights after playing for the Leafs was a neat situation, since it seemed as though everyone had watched the game. That's when the attention really started for me. Being drafted seventh overall and playing in the World Junior Championship had certainly made more hockey fans aware of me—but after playing a single game for the Leafs, everything took off.

In every city where the Knights played, there were people who came out to watch me on the ice. With Maple Leafs fans in every single city across Canada, it seemed as if everywhere we went, there were Leafs jerseys in the crowd. And at first that was very cool. It's sweet when you're a young player and people are asking for pictures and autographs.

But I had to bear down a bit more because that's when everyone zeroed in on me. I felt the pressure to perform. It was a privilege, of course, and I was so thankful for it. Yet it was also a taste of the attention that comes with being a Leaf.

After a while I struggled to deal with it. The attention became a distraction and a little annoying. When I was out for dinner with my family, we couldn't eat without someone coming up and asking for a picture. It was a bit of a rollercoaster ride.

Still, I played well amid the attention. That was my best year in the OHL, leading the Knights with thirty-five goals and ninety-five points. I also played with more of an edge than I had before, racking up 105 penalty minutes—nearly double my previous high. And I was named for the OHL's player of the year award alongside Taylor Hall and Tyler Seguin, who were the consensus picks to go first and second overall in the upcoming NHL draft. (Seguin also took the Red Tilson Trophy after putting up 106 points in 63 games for the Plymouth Whalers.)

When the Knights finished second in the Western Conference behind the Windsor Spitfire, I hoped to be part of one last deep run in the playoffs with the franchise that had meant so much to me as a kid and as a player trying to make it to the NHL.

We walked over Guelph in the first round. After that series I led all playoff scorers, with fourteen points in five games. I was feeling pretty good.

Then we met the Kitchener Rangers in the conference semifinal. The Rangers had improved dramatically after rebuilding for a year following our Memorial Cup run. They were led by seventeen-year-old Jeff Skinner, who would go seventh overall in that year's NHL draft. The team also had a talented sixteen-year-old Swede named Gabriel Landeskog, who the Colorado Avalanche would select second overall in the 2011 NHL draft.

It was a dogfight of a series, one that, fittingly, went to seven games. As we beat the Rangers at the Aud to force that final game, I got into a chirping match with a group of Rangers fans while I was sitting in the penalty box—but then another group of Rangers fans chimed in to back me up. It was nice to know that no matter what, I'd always have some support in Kitchener.

We played Game 7 at home in front of nine thousand people. It felt as if we had the momentum as our fans let the Rangers know whose building they were in. But early in the second period the Rangers informed us that they didn't care. They scored five straight goals to take a stranglehold in the game and effectively finish off our year. We lost 8–3, which was a bitter way to end my junior career. But as much as it stung, it was kind of nice to see my old team move on. I shared a few kind words with Rangers coach Steve Spott, who'd been an assistant coach during my two years with the club.

Before I left the ice, I took a moment to reflect on what it had all meant. London was the place where hockey first came to life for me. It was the city where a Lebanese immigrant who didn't speak English could offer his family possibilities he hadn't had. It was where my father learned to dream, and where he learned what it took to realize those dreams. It was where those lessons had been passed on to me. Now my grandfather sat in the corner by the glass, watching his grandson reach for a dream that would have been unimaginable a generation before.

I stepped off the ice one last time—defeated, disappointed—but grateful. London was the place where this crazy journey had become possible. It was and always would be home.

8

GETTING AHEAD OF MYSELF

THE SUMMER BEFORE MY FIRST full season in Toronto, I rented a condo a few blocks away from the Air Canada Centre. I was confident that I'd be playing with the Leafs that year, worst-case scenario being that I'd spend some time with the Marlies in the American Hockey League. Either way, I'd be downtown. And it was exciting to move into my own place for the first time. I got it all set up, with new furniture and everything. It was a great spot.

I was nineteen, ready to embark on my life as a professional athlete.

In hindsight, I may have gotten ahead of myself.

There was a lot of expectation surrounding me as a seventh overall pick. That expectation only grew after the success I'd had during my first Leafs training camp, my showing at the World Juniors, and the season I'd had with London.

I spent most of the summer working out with conditioning coach Anthony Belza. We worked together five times a week, adding more than fifteen pounds of muscle. I'd bulked up to almost 190 pounds in time for training camp. My size had been the biggest concern previously, so I felt I'd done what I needed to do to address that.

I had a bold personality as a young person. I felt pretty good about myself. And at that time it rubbed some people the wrong way.

The media was already describing me as "cocky." Management bristled at the confidence I showed in my ability. I was accused of sulking after the decision to send me back to junior following my first training camp. And I was criticized in the press for being "entitled" after I remarked how I was looking forward to buying my first Ferrari. I was nineteen. I *was* looking forward to buying my first Ferrari. Who wouldn't?

But I didn't think of myself as cocky. I just wanted to handle myself as though I believed I belonged. And there wasn't much consideration given as to why I carried myself the way I did. Growing up, I always thought no one would believe in me if I didn't believe in myself. As I've said, I hadn't come from a typical hockey background; no one in my family had played the sport before me. And ever since I was a kid people had hurled racist insults at me from the stands and on the ice. In effect, I was told that I didn't belong in their game, that it was a game for white kids.

And so my confidence was a callus, built up in response to those factors. I believed in myself because I knew others didn't. I was confident because of their doubt. I had to be.

But the fact that I come from a different background than other guys doesn't explain everything about me. It's not like I would have been a saint if I didn't have a Middle Eastern name on the back of my sweater. I am the kind of guy I am, no matter what people think about my last name or my religion. But if you take a take a scrappy kid, add even a little bit of racism or whatever it is that makes people think you can't look different or do things differently, and tell that kid he can't do things his way, chances are you're only going to increase the scrappiness. I know everyone faces their own challenges. People tell some kids they can't make it because they are too small, or whatever. I'm not the only guy in the NHL who has ever had to overcome other people's outdated ideas. The thing is, how many guys like Marty St. Louis gave up because they were told they didn't look like other players? How many guys with darker skin? We will never know—but we do know that we missed out on some great talent. I also know that I was never going to take no for an answer. If anyone thought anything about me was going to get in my way, my number one goal was to prove them wrong. Was that cockiness? If so, all I can say is you don't make it in the NHL without cockiness, and the league needs more of it.

I don't think many people in hockey at the time could have understood that. Certainly not the old guard who decided how hockey players should act. In the NHL there was a vanilla way of doing things, especially for rookies. When I came into the league my confidence was viewed as a character flaw. But I knew it was one of my most valuable weapons. And nowadays that's what teams look for. They want a guy to come in and think he can make some noise right off the bat. But from the beginning, I was kind of shunned for being overly assured.

That wasn't my perception.

Ahead of camp, I told reporters that I believed I could be a centre on one of the Leafs' top two lines that season. "I feel like I'm ready to take on that responsibility," I said. "Nothing is set in stone. I'm pretty confident."

I was telling the truth. No one appreciated it. That would turn out to be a pattern.

IT'S AN UNDERSTATEMENT TO SAY that things got off to a rocky start in Toronto. Looking back on it now, there were moments where I was a bit of an idiot. I just didn't know the ropes. I was coming from junior hockey and I hadn't played pro yet. It took me some time to learn.

Before one of my first pre-season games with the Leafs, I walked into the locker room wearing a pair of large black Beats headphones. I used to hype myself up with music. It was a form of energy for me. I was just rocking out, trying to get in the zone. Everyone was probably looking at me like "what the fuck is this kid doing?"

There was some rule that we couldn't wear headphones in the locker room.

The old school mentality was still very pervasive when I first came into the league. Things were a lot harsher than they are today.

The guys let me do my thing to get ready, but after the game they laid into me about wearing the goofy giant headphones. I wasn't trying to be arrogant, but I thought they were crazy. What was the big deal?

The next day when I got to the rink, Burkie called me into his office. He looked pissed.

"Don't ever wear those fucking headphones anywhere close to the arena ever again," he said. "I don't care what the fuck you do with them, but don't ever even consider wearing them around the arena again."

I honestly hadn't meant to offend anybody, but clearly I'd struck a nerve with the veteran guys in the locker room. They were probably wondering who the fuck I thought I was.

Okay. Message delivered. I tossed the Beats away and stopped listening to my own music before the game. I had to settle for whatever was playing in the locker room, which wasn't my cup of tea, but I didn't have a choice.

My pre-season wasn't great. I felt a lot of pressure to earn a spot with the Leafs right away, and that got into my head a little bit. I didn't feel natural out there. I spent time playing along Kris Versteeg and Colby Armstrong—two great guys, but we didn't really connect on the ice. There's a big adjustment when you make a leap to the NHL, and I understood that. Yet while some went so far as to wonder if I needed to return to junior for another season, I believed I was better off playing in the NHL environment and figuring it out.

I went minus three with a point in our first three pre-season games and was left off the roster for our fourth against the Buffalo Sabres. I tried to stay positive. "I think physically and mentally, I'm all there," I told reporters after that 3–1 loss to the Sabres. "With a little more practice, I think I'll be pretty sharp. So, just given the opportunity, I'm going to hopefully cash in on it."

Late in training camp Burke was openly critical of my play. During a conference call with the press, he even questioned whether I deserved to start the season with the Leafs. "This is not uncommon at all with a young player—that there's a lot of hype, maybe a lot of pressure with a hometown kid," Burke said. "Whatever the reasons, we haven't lost faith at all with Nazem Kadri. But his play right now indicates that he's not ready at all to contribute at this level . . . He's not anywhere near what we had hoped for or expected. I don't know why that is. And he's running out of time. His comments seem to indicate that he thinks he has a lot more time. But he's running out of time here."

Leafs coach Ron Wilson was just as hard on me. He always had kind of a matter-of-fact way of sending a message, and he didn't hold back when it came to his thoughts about me and my disappointing performance through training camp. He criticized my commitment to defensive zone coverage and told the press that I'd have to show improvement before earning a full-time job in the NHL. "He's had lots of opportunities to make an impression," Ron said. "He's got to realize the situation he's in and get the job done, not talk his way out of how he's played up to this point. He's got to actually do it."

The comments were tough to take, but I wasn't about to wilt. Early on as a player I'd learned to be mentally tough. I had one more thing to prove. And I proved it.

"You can't just melt when someone criticizes you," I said when reporters asked about it. I was right about that. Mental toughness is something that every athlete needs. You want a guy with the balls to say "fuck you." But saying "fuck you" without actually listening can slow you down too. It can prevent you from learning.

Wilson hinted that our last pre-season game against the Senators would be my last chance to show the team that I deserved a spot on the roster. But I was able to take all the negative things people had said about me and use it as fuel on the ice. I wanted to make people eat their words. It was an "I'll show you" kind of approach. I was good at it. That attitude was a blessing—and at times a curse. It helped make me who I am today.

Right after Wilson said that, I went out and showed the team that I belonged. I put together a two-goal, one-assist evening in a 4–3 win over the Ottawa Senators, in which I was named first star of the game. I played on the top line alongside Tyler Bozak and Phil Kessel. We played well together, and I thought we had a lot of potential.

It didn't matter. Afterward, the team carried the same tune.

It was clear that they didn't think I'd earned a spot in the top six and that they didn't intend to keep me in the press box when I could be playing in the minors. The team felt more comfortable with Tyler and Mikhail Grabovski centring the first and second line.

I WAS MAD ABOUT BEING sent down to the minors to start the season. That was obvious to everyone. But there was also a lot going on behind the scenes that people didn't know about.

I'd settled into my downtown condo when Burke said he wanted me to live with a billet family in Oakville. The father in the family was a cop. The team couldn't have been more blatant about wanting to keep close tabs on me.

I objected. My apartment was right downtown and I didn't want to commute all the way from Oakville when I could just walk to the Air Canada Centre. Plus, I was already paying rent and had a year-long lease. And again, I was nineteen, living in the city. I didn't want to be babysat by strangers in the suburbs. But Burkie wasn't interested in hearing my case.

"Can you guys at least pay for my lease?" I asked, knowing that I'd be wasting a bunch of cash on a place where the team wouldn't even let me stay.

No, Burke said. They wouldn't.

That pissed me off. But *whatever*. I packed an overnight bag and drove to the billet house around eight that night. I met the whole family. Lovely folks. Nothing against them. They seemed like genuinely great people. They gave me a tour of the house, showed me my room, and gave me a set of keys. They told me to think of their home as my own and seemed willing to go out of their way just to make me feel welcome.

I slept in my brand-new bedroom that night. The next morning I packed up and left the house around eight for practice. I never went back.

I called the cop and let him know that I planned to be downtown a lot, so they probably wouldn't see me very much. That bought me a bit of time. No one said anything for a while. I guess the cop chose not to rat me out to the team. But on my way to a game early in the season, I stepped into the elevator and one of the Leafs' assistant coaches was standing there. He lived in the same building.

Fuck.

"Aren't you supposed to be somewhere else?" he said.

"Oh, yeah—yeah," I said. "I just came to pick up a few things."

He didn't buy it.

Burkie called me into his office after that. "What the fuck are you doing?" he said.

I was pretty sure it was a rhetorical question. After all, I'd been caught red-handed.

I tried to explain my side of it. I'd already paid for the place, and I was way more comfortable in my own space, close to the arena. I knew myself well enough to know that living with a family would throw me off. I rhymed off as many reasons as I could before Burke had heard enough.

"Fuck it," he said. "Just come ready to play."

9
STILL GRINDING

THE WAFFLES WERE A BIZARRE sign of the times. To this day, I still don't understand it. Why waffles—and why Eggos, specifically? Everyone was frustrated by the way the team was playing through the first half of the 2010–2011 season.

Toronto had missed the playoffs for five straight years, the longest streak in franchise history. But in this season the team started off promisingly, with a four-game winning streak. Then, through November, we dropped eight in a row. By December it looked like we were on our way to extending that playoff drought to six. The fans seemed to have already written off the season.

Early that month, after we'd lost 4–1 to the Philadelphia Flyers, some clown tossed a handful of waffles over the glass. None of us really paid that much attention to it. Weird things get thrown from the stands sometimes. But we were asked about it after the game, and just like that, waffles became a symbol for our shitty play.

Naturally there were a lot of questions.

"I don't know what this waffle business is all about," I told a scrum of reporters. "Did they bring 'em, or buy them at the concession?"

One guy online, claiming to be the initial waffle tosser, wrote that he did it because we "needed to wake up and eat some breakfast," which was one of the stranger insults I've heard.

Later that month, as we were getting trashed by the Atlanta Thrashers, another fan tossed waffles on the ice during the game, forcing the play to stop. He was arrested for mischief. That guy told ESPN that if you drop the "w" you get "awful"—which was a bit better.

The press ran with puns about the teams waffling. Fans ran with jokes and memes online. Waffles were everywhere. It was ridiculous, but it reflected the way fans felt about the state of our team.

It was a challenging time to be a Leaf. And for me, it was a challenging time to be a Leaf-slash-Marlie. I'd been sent to the minors right out of training camp, but had since been called up for several stints with the main club as I fought to prove myself to the team's brass.

Of course I disagreed with the decision to hold me back in the minors. Burke said they wanted to give me some more experience playing alongside men. I felt that was bullshit. But that's how it goes in professional hockey. The only way I could change their minds was by playing better.

And I played well with the Marlies. I knew there was only so much I could gain from being held back at that level. But then I'd be called up to the Leafs and wouldn't be able to find my footing. I'd struggle and then be sent back down.

In the first part of the season I was called up for seventeen games with the Leafs, mostly on the wing. I struggled throughout, scoring no goals and racking up just six assists during that time. Even though I felt prepared, I just couldn't seem to find my rhythm on the ice. In late November I was bumped up to the top line, between Kessel and

Clarke MacArthur. It was a big opportunity for me. But when I was younger, I let things roll off my back pretty easily and didn't stress about much. I'd known Phil for a little bit at the time, but not a whole lot. He and I were kind of similar in that neither of us took things too seriously.

I remember seeing my name on the board next to his, announcing that I'd been bumped up. Later, Phil came up to me in the locker room.

"Wow," he said. "You hit the lottery today man. You're playing with me."

The way he said it was so funny. I was almost in tears.

"Yeah, I'm excited," I said.

I walked away and laughed it off. Phil and I developed a great relationship after that. He's quite the character. But at the time, on the ice together, nothing really worked. It wasn't just me; we weren't playing well as a group. Many factors contributed to this, but the bottom line was that we just weren't a very good team.

Whether I should be playing with the Leafs was a big topic for the media and fans throughout those first couple months of the season. Some people seemed to think I just needed a chance to show what I was capable of, while others wrote me off completely. My play was put under a microscope, which is something I'd expected in a market like Toronto. I knew enough not to let it get to me, but it's tough when you've just turned twenty and you hear people on the radio criticizing your work ethic and calling you cocky. I was criticized in the media for not sufficiently "embracing the game," whatever the hell that means. Some people argued that the team had been overly generous in the time they'd given me with the Leafs.

Others were behind me. Don Cherry continued to be one of my most vocal supporters—pretty much every time he discussed the Leafs, it seemed as though he called for me to come up. I appreciated

Grapes putting a little extra pressure on the organization. In fact I was loving every second of it, because it just didn't seem as if the team had my back.

Behind the scenes, management was harsh. Even though Burkie took jabs at me in the press, it didn't really bother me because that was always his style. I knew he believed in me. But there were people in his management group who didn't. We didn't get along that well. They'd pegged me as a problem from day one, criticizing me from the moment I arrived in training camp that year.

We had so many meetings about what was wrong with me as a player. Meeting after meeting after meeting they talked about what a shitty hockey player I was. It was brutal.

And they were always on me about my self-assurance. "Why are you so confident?" I remember being asked, more than once. "You've done nothing."

At first I tried not to let it get to me. These were old-school hockey guys who came from an era when players weren't supposed to have any kind of personality or sense of individuality. You were expected to fall in line and pay your dues. Nowadays they want young players to be confident. They want you to feel like you belong. It's the complete opposite. I don't know if these guys were just behind the times. But the shit they pulled wouldn't fly in the NHL today. It's an entirely backward mentality.

It was as if it bothered them that it bothered me that I'd been sent to the minors. But why would a team want a player to be okay with that? Didn't they *want* me to be upset about it? It was as if they felt that believing in yourself was a character flaw. Still, as critical as they were about the way I was playing, no one was harder on me than myself. That's something they probably couldn't see.

I remember leaving a couple of those meetings absolutely stunned. I was just a twenty-year-old kid and they were basically saying I didn't have what it takes to play in the show. And this was the team that had drafted me. They had an interest in at least trying to believe in me, but they couldn't even bring themselves to do that.

It should have been discouraging, but actually it just really pissed me off. Again, I used it as fuel.

"I'm going to shove it up their asses," I told myself. "They're going to be gone and I'm still going to be here."

I played it off on the outside. Right before the new year, after I'd been demoted to the Marlies again, reporters heard about a meeting that assistant GM Dave Poulin and Marlie GM Claude Loiselle had with me, in which they drilled me on how I was approaching the game.

"It was a bit bitter, but at the same time that's the way it is," I told Mark Zwolinski of the *Toronto Star* before a Marlies game at Ricoh Coliseum. "You have to be able to take that, and I can take it. I've been around hockey long enough to know how these things work. I know what I have to do to get back and I have things to work on."

But I was incredibly frustrated. Our team wasn't very good, but I was still being sent up and down when I could be developing as an NHL player playing against the best in the world every night. I was very confused about it. I felt I should have been there and that I was kind of being screwed around. I was definitely good enough to play with the Leafs. I also knew that I had a lot to learn. By no means did I think I was the perfect player. Believing in myself meant that I believed I could be a much better player than I was, that I wasn't going to let it get me down. I'd grind it out and figure it out as I always did. I didn't need these dinosaurs giving me lessons on what I should think about myself.

That season I played forty-four games with the Marlies under coach Dallas Eakins. During that time I scored seventeen goals and forty-one points—and I felt that was enough for me.

IN MID-MARCH THE LEAFS CALLED me up again. It was then that things started to finally click. I was playing the way I knew I could.

We faced the Bruins four games into the call-up. I played probably my strongest game ever up to that point. During one sequence I dumped the puck out of our zone instead of trying to carry it out, which is something Ron Wilson had been on me about. After that I fought for possession along the boards in the Bruins' zone, keeping the puck in their end. I dropped back to cover the line after defenceman Carl Gunnarsson pinched. Then, when the puck came back to me near the blue line, I wristed it on goal; the puck deflected off one of the Bruins' helmets and bounced into the net—my first NHL goal. It certainly wasn't the prettiest, but I was happy to take it. It was going on my wall regardless.

After the game, it was a relief to finally answer questions about how well I'd played rather than how poorly. I was asked how, a couple of decades into the future, I'd recount the story of my first NHL goal.

"I'll probably say I walked past a few guys and went backhand shelf," I said after our 5–2 win.

I believed I was evolving as a player, and adapting to the stronger play and faster pace of the NHL. My time with the big club was much more valuable to me than playing in the AHL. I could only hope the Leafs' management would see that too.

"I think it's a maturity thing," I told the scrum, pointing to my last game. "My defensive plays and how I played with the puck on the walls were pretty exceptional. So I just have to keep it up. I think what people were concerned about was my defensive skills, so I think that's something that I can be proud of."

WE SAT NEAR THE BOTTOM of the standings through most of the season, but then went on a bit of a run through its final stretch, making a last-ditch push for the playoffs. The fans kept their waffles at home. It was fun to be part of it, and to show fans the kind of player I actually was.

Even Wilson praised me, in his own sarcastic, backhanded way. "You want to call it maturity?" he said when reporters asked him about my play a week later. "Well, I guess he's matured a little bit. He's been humbled by playing most of the year in the minors. He was focused on offence and standing around and little dinky plays that don't work in the NHL."

Ronny never held back. But he also showed confidence in me. The next day our game in Boston went to a shootout, with an extra point hanging in the balance. We desperately needed the win over the Bruins to keep our faint playoff hopes alive. Then Wilson called on me to shoot a second. Neither side had managed to score before it was my turn.

I felt the nerves as I stood at centre ice, staring at Tim Thomas, one of the best goalies in the league. The game was on the line.

"Just trust your hands," I told myself. "You've done this a million times before."

But never on this stage—and never with so much at stake.

I touched the puck and moved toward the goal. It seemed to take forever. I stickhandled in close on Thomas, then quickly deked to my backhand. He reached back with his pad and glove and flicked the puck. It felt like one of those slow-motion scenes from *The Mighty*

Ducks movies. The puck crossed the line just above Thomas's outstretched arm, hit the net, and fell to the ice.

I felt a rush of relief and joy, both of which had been in such short supply all season.

Not long after that, I watched from the bench as James Reimer turned aside Rich Peverley to secure the shootout win. It was the best feeling I'd ever experienced in the NHL. Not only was this our fifth win in six games, but the goal I'd scored was the biggest of my young NHL career.

Three nights later Leafs fans filled Scotiabank Place in Ottawa, turning our away game against the Senators into what felt like home-ice advantage. In the first period I scored my third goal of the season when Craig Anderson flubbed a pass from behind the Senators' goal right onto my stick behind the net. I fired a pass toward Phil Kessel in front, but the puck bounced off Anderson's skate as he scrambled to get back and then deflected into the net. Another ugly goal, but another one I'd happily keep. That put us up 2–0, after which we held on for a 4–2 win.

We ended up falling just short of the playoffs. Still, we managed to reignite the fans who came along for the late-season ride with us. I finished my rookie season with three goals and twelve points in twenty-nine appearances with the Leafs. It was a forgettable stat line, but more importantly, I'd shown through the final stretch of the season that I could be a key contributor to the club.

We were the second-youngest team in the NHL and chockful of rising talent, with draft picks like Luke Schenn and me starting to come into our own. Late in the season we'd picked up prospect defenceman Jake Gardiner along with Joffrey Lupul from Anaheim. Phil Kessel was one of the most lethal young scorers in the league. James Reimer was emerging as a reliable number-one tender. Dion

Phaneuf was a rock-solid captain. The rebuild was well underway, and I felt there could be something special on the horizon for us.

At the end of the season, Wilson claimed boldly that he believed we were just two or three pieces away from being a Stanley Cup contender. Not just a playoff team—a contender for the Cup.

And despite my differences with management and the frustrations of that first full season as a pro, I believed it too.

10
A MOVIE I'LL NEVER WATCH

DO YOU KNOW THE MOVIE *Bull Durham*? The one from the late eighties, where Tim Robbins plays a young pitcher named Nuke LaLoosh?

He's talented but super cocky. He's said to have a "million-dollar arm but a five-cent head." LaLoosh has the potential to become a major league talent but is wasting away in the minor leagues, so a veteran minor leaguer named Crash Davis—played by Kevin Costner—is sent down to the Durham Bulls to help LaLoosh find his game and avoid the same mistakes he made.

I've heard it's a decent sports flick, but I've never seen it. I had to look up that summary online because I've vowed never to watch it.

MY THIRD SEASON WITH THE Leafs began as a frustrating game of déjà vu. I'd played well with them to finish out the previous season, but management was still noncommittal about my future with the club.

So it felt like a make-or-break camp for me that September 2011. I had two seasons to go on my entry-level deal, but if I couldn't find a way to stick with the Leafs, my time with the team might be near its end.

I did my part. I came to camp leaner and stronger than ever, shredding away body fat. I was a much quicker player. I'd worked hard on those elements of the game the team had asked me to address. I'd cut out the risky plays. And I was using my weight much more effectively, tossing my body around, playing physically at both ends of the ice.

Burkie still took his half-hearted shots at me. During training camp he told reporters that I was "dangerous with the puck, but sometimes for the wrong team." Yet it was obvious to anyone paying attention that I'd put together the best camp I'd had with the Leafs.

But the team made it clear that I wasn't a lock for a roster spot.

"It will be the same as last year," Wilson said. "If someone plays better than Kadri, he'll start in the minors."

That was fine with me because I knew I could demonstrate how much I deserved to be there. Meanwhile they seemed set on making sure I knew that I had no special status as a first-round pick, that I'd have to work as hard or harder than all their other prospects.

I was determined to do that anyway.

I was often asked about my attitude—about whether, over my previous two seasons with the Leafs, I'd learned any lessons about appearing too confident. But I made sure everyone knew that I was the same kid who'd refused to stop believing in himself.

"I don't think that's worn off. I don't think it should wear off. I still have that kind of swagger," I told the *Toronto Star*'s Rosie DiManno. "I still have that confidence. Anyone, to play in this league, needs that. You can't have low self-esteem to play in the NHL."

Throughout camp I was pitted against Joe Colborne—who at six-five and 218 pounds was a much different player than I was. Matt

Frattin, a rookie centre coming out of the University of North Dakota, was also in the mix. We all worked our asses off trying to earn that spot on the final roster.

I was as clear as ever about my intentions. "I've had my little stint in the American Hockey League and I did very well," I said when asked whether I needed another year of experience with the Marlies. "It's time to man up and play in the NHL."

By the time training camp neared its end, it was all but determined that I'd earned a position with the big club—which is when I injured my left knee during a pre-season game against the Ottawa Senators. It was just a sprained medial collateral ligament, but it put me on the sidelines for the Leafs' season opener.

For the third straight year I wouldn't start the regular season with the Maple Leafs.

"This whole summer is not going to go to waste just because of a three-week injury," I said. "When I'm a hundred percent ready, I think I'll be able to hop in and kind of play an impact role and hopefully contribute to my team right away."

I sat out the first four games of the season as I recovered. The expectation was that I'd join the club as soon as I was cleared to play. But when I returned to the ice for my first practice, I was placed with a group of extras.

In mid-October, shortly after I'd turned twenty-one, the Leafs briefly assigned me to the Marlies for some tune-up games before calling me back up for my first game of the season. But a week later, after a few games with the Leafs, I was sent back down.

It was a demoralizing, never-ending rollercoaster.

Returning to the Marlies set me back mentally. It was finally starting to wear on me. I carried so much hope and expectation that to be knocked back down again almost defeated me. And so I struggled on the ice. I was fighting the puck. I just couldn't play my game. My confidence—which everyone had been so quick to call cockiness—took a major hit.

But after that slow start with the Marlies, I managed to push away my disappointment and find my stride again. In November I was named the AHL's player of the month. By early December I'd scored six goals and added eleven assists in fourteen games. We had a very good squad, which went on a six-game winning streak through that time.

Later that month I returned to the Leafs and scored my first goal of the season—a game winner against Buffalo—but just the fourth of my NHL career. Three seasons after being drafted, this was not where I'd hoped to be. I struggled again, putting up just a single point in ten games. Then in February, after six weeks in the show, I was demoted once more.

That year the Leafs fell out of playoff contention again, which further angered the fan base. And again, one of the biggest debates in social media and on sports radio was what the team should be doing with me.

"It's frustrating," I told Sean Fitzgerald. "It's pretty frustrating to watch them struggle and me thinking I could help . . . I have all the faith in myself. I know that I can be a game-changer, and I just hope they see that, too."

THEY COULDN'T SEE IT, THOUGH. They made that very clear behind closed doors.

One meeting was particularly memorable. Several members of the team's management sat in the room with just me. Outnumbered as

I was, I didn't say much, and anyway by that point there was little use trying to defend myself. This time I just took it on the chin.

They'd printed out a list of first-round draft picks who'd turned out to be busts in the NHL. One asshole read me the entire list. It was obvious that the team felt I was drifting into bust territory.

I couldn't believe it. Here I was, in my third year with the franchise, and they still seemed determined to make sure drafting me had been a mistake.

This was the kind of cruelty and bitterness that happened off-stage. Why are they telling a kid this? Especially a kid in whom they'd invested so much money.

After they brought out that list, I was done with them. I mean, I still wanted to be a Leaf. I hadn't asked for a trade and I never would. But as far as I was concerned, I had no respect for the people running the franchise beneath Burke.

It wasn't Burkie himself. We had a good relationship. Burkie and I got along well; he'd always chat with me and was pretty encouraging. But the people around him had all kinds of issues with me. They were screwing me around and making it seem as though I was the problem.

As they went on during that meeting, I once again told myself I'd be with the Leafs way longer than any of the men who were sitting in the room calling me a bust. That I'd prove these guys wrong and get them canned in the process. That was my mentality. I went to another level.

At the end of the meeting one of them told me there was a movie he felt I needed to watch. I wanted to spit in his face. He wrote down the name of the movie and handed me the piece of paper.

I looked down and read the title: *Bull Durham*.

I'd never heard of it. As I turned to walk out of the room, I crumpled up the piece of paper and tossed it in the trash can beside the door.

To this day, I've never watched that movie. Not once. I never will. It's a lifelong boycott for me.

11
FINDING MY GAME

IN EARLY MARCH 2012, AMID a tailspin in which the Leafs lost ten of eleven games, Ron Wilson was fired. Randy Carlyle was hired to replace him. As a former Leafs defenceman who'd won a Stanley Cup as head coach of the Anaheim Ducks alongside Brian Burke, Carlyle brought a new vision to our rebuilding franchise. I was hopeful that the change might open up better avenues for me with the club.

Later that month, as an emergency call-up to the Leafs, I redirected a Jake Gardiner shot to put us up 2–0 in the second period. Then, in overtime, I scored in the shootout on legendary goaltender Martin Brodeur.

It was only my twentieth game of the season with the Leafs. I'd have one more before being sent back to the Marlies, where I'd play forty-eight games that season, putting in the time the Leafs so passionately felt I needed. And I finished the AHL season with eighteen goals and twenty-two assists in those forty-eight games, once again showing that I was ready to move to the next level.

The demotion held another silver lining. While the Leafs failed to make the playoffs for the eighth straight year, the Marlies went on a huge playoff run to the Calder Cup final that June. And I did well through the playoffs, showing off my ability to play a gritty game, to be a pain in the ass for our opponents. The excitement around the "Baby Leafs" rekindled some hope for fans who'd endured so much disappointment with the big-league club. We were swept in the final by a very good Norfolk Admirals squad that had players like Richard Panik, Alex Killorn, Tyler Johnson, and Ondrej Palat. But the experience was invaluable for me. Battling through four playoff series at that level was the kind of testing ground that does so much for a player's development. I'd had that with the Kitchener Rangers before joining the London Knights. It helps you understand just what it takes to become one of the last teams standing.

Through my first three seasons as a pro I'd spent the vast majority of my time in the minors, with just fifty NHL games to my name. But I remained optimistic that things were about to change.

I began the off-season with a singular mindset: to continue getting stronger, with a specific focus on my lower body. And I went right to the best, working my ass off with Gary Roberts, who'd become a renowned strength coach after retiring from the NHL. Gary had initiated things the previous spring when he joined the discourse around my playing time, asking on Twitter whether Burke would let me stay with the big team if I trained with him. I saw the tweet, figured it was worth a shot, and went through Gary's boot camp all summer, preparing to attend a Leafs training camp for the fourth time. Gary had me in there at seven a.m. every single day. It was an absolute pain in the ass. I lived downtown and his gym was way out in Scarborough. I was up at six every morning, battling traffic trying to get to the gym. But I took it very seriously and learned a lot from Gary. The man was as intense in the gym as he was on the ice when he played. He taught me the importance of taking care of my body, and he put me onto acupuncture, which was something I didn't know about at the time. I hated needles. But he pushed me through that, and it paid off. Gary was always a champ. I'd get to the gym, and he'd already have been there for an hour and a half, just leaking sweat. Completely drenched, like he just dove into a pool. As a young guy, I was impressed. "This is how this guy is living?" I thought. "Damn." I learned so much about work ethics and commitment from him.

When I arrived at camp that September I felt great. I was noticeably faster and much more explosive, especially on my first couple of steps. I was able to immediately create distance from the opposing player. It was the best I'd ever felt on the ice. My confidence had returned. I knew I was playing the best hockey of my life.

And I ended up having a monster camp, making it pretty much impossible for the Leafs to demote me. The only problem was that a labour dispute between the Players Association and the NHL had led to a lockout, which started on September 15, 2012.

Right when I'd all but assured myself a consistent role in the NHL, there was no season to play in. Perfect.

DURING THE NHL LOCKOUT THAT FALL I returned to the Marlies (since the American League continued operating), and of course this time there was nothing I could do about it.

On the first day of Marlies camp, my name started trending on Twitter when Marlies coach Dallas Eakins publicly criticized my eating habits and the level of fat I carried. Eakins claimed my body fat ratio was among the worst of all the guys on the team.

"That's unacceptable," he told the *Toronto Star* in an interview that set off a firestorm.

I was surprised by the comments, because my body fat ratio was much better than it had been the previous season; plus, during training camp I'd performed much better on every fitness test I was put through. Meanwhile I'd spent the first couple years as a pro being told I was too small. Now I was too fat? What did the guy want?

"That's the easiest part coming into camp—eating correctly and training correctly," Eakins said in the interview. "I think he's probably improved a little bit on the ice. His diet is not where it should be."

Look, I did hate vegetables. There is no way around that. I just did. But I was being conscious of my diet, especially under the guidance of Roberts, who is a nutrition freak.

"I'm still a young guy," I said in response. "I'm slowly learning how to be a pro and what types of food to put in my body . . . I'm a pretty picky eater. I don't like too many things. The squash and the spinach, these healthy dressings you've got to put on your salad, I'm not a huge fan of. I learned these are the things I have to put in my body. As time goes on, I'm sure my taste buds will react positively."

The next day the front page of the *Toronto Sun* ran a photo of me with the headline "FAT . . . SO?," insinuating that I was out of shape, but that I still had talent. It was clever, actually. I couldn't tell if it was a compliment or not. But I'd never imagined being called a fatso on the front page of a newspaper. Now I can look back on it and laugh, but it wasn't as funny back then.

I remember thinking "What the fuck? I'm being called fat by one of the biggest newspapers in the biggest city in Canada. I'm twenty years old!"

I was down on myself that day. That doubt started to creep in. I'd worked out with Gary Roberts that summer and felt good about myself. Now everyone was talking about my weight and this huge headline. It was an absolute mess. Looking back, I can see how ridiculous it is to call anyone in an NHL locker room fat. Are you kidding me? Do you think you can play this game and be out of shape? Anyone that isn't playing pro hockey and comments on a player's fitness has no idea what they are talking about.

Think about what that does to a twenty-year-old kid. I had to learn to shrug that off. (Don Cherry was one of the few people who defended me at the time, which I really appreciated.) I didn't respond to the headline or any of the commentary. I just let it all go. It was a moment where I had to learn a difficult lesson about not letting the outside noise get to me. You just fuel the fire if you respond, so you have to just let it fizzle out.

You don't see all the criticism, but you're aware of the main storyline about you. It's impossible not to. Everyone sees it, but how much they pay attention to it is a whole different story.

I tried not to let Eakins's comments eat at me. Anyway I'd already started thinking differently about how I approached nutrition and training. In the past I'd taken the old-school approach, in which the season was for hockey, the off-season for working out. I was still wrapping my head around the consistent commitment it took to succeed as a professional athlete. But now I understood the importance of maintaining strength throughout the season and of training with a more hockey-focused program over the summer. And I knew it would be only a matter of time before everyone around me saw the results.

People had a field day with Eakins's comments. (Although once again Don Cherry came to my defence. On Twitter he accused the team of trying to destroy me with public criticism. "I have never in my life seen a kid treated like Nazem Kadri by the Leafs," he wrote.)

And rather than get upset, I let my play speak for me. I put my head down and grinded through the next three weeks of camp, knowing I was in a position to show the organization how wrong it had been about me. I continued to play the best hockey of my life.

A few weeks later, Eakins walked the comments back.

"He's made great, great strides," he said. "His diet. I see him in the gym all the time. I'm getting positive reports from our fitness guy [Mark Fitzgerald]. He's upped his pace in practice."

But Eakins also defended the approach that he and the organization had taken with me over the previous three seasons. Two years ago, he said, I needed to work on not turning over pucks and recognizing danger.

"And he got way better at that," Eakins conceded. "Last year, I said we need this guy to make a bigger commitment to D-zone coverage. And he did. He got better. This year, I said he needs a better commitment to the way he eats, and people went crazy."

Again, I didn't let it get to me. I kept playing hard, knowing I was on the edge of breaking into the NHL once the lockout ended. So when the players and the league came to an agreement to salvage half the season that January, I was ready to dare the Leafs not to keep me. By that time I had twenty-six points in twenty-seven games with the Marlies—and had played my last game in the minors.

Where I would play was such a dominant media story and the focus of so many vocal fans that I don't think the Leafs could have kept me down for another season even if they wanted to. Plus I had another exceptional camp as the team rushed to prepare for a shortened season that winter.

Then, in early January, right before the season kicked off, Brian Burke was fired as Leafs president and general manager. It was hard to see the guy who'd drafted me get the boot. I'd since learned a lot about the darker realities of professional sports, and although Burkie was tough on me, it was in a way I respected. I knew he wanted to see me succeed in the NHL.

"It's disappointing for a man who works so hard and dedicated so much of his time to his team, but that being said it's part of the business," I said the morning we learned he'd been dismissed. "It's not all on his shoulders. He's the one who suffered the consequences but we take it upon ourselves."

At camp, I was finally ready to be the player Burke believed I could be when he'd drafted me back in 2009. And this time, after three years of disappointment, I forced my way into a top-six role and refused to look back.

WHEN CAMP ENDED I WAS named to the Leafs' opening roster for the first time. Playing the Montreal Canadiens at the Bell Centre in our season opener felt like a full-circle moment—it had been three long years since I'd sat in those stands and heard my name called. I had no idea then how much the team would doubt my ability, no concept of how much difficulty lay ahead. But I could still hear my family cheering from the top section of the arena. And I was still determined to make them proud.

In the first period I scored the first goal of our season, taking a pass from Phil Kessel on the power play and firing a shot past Carey Price. We went on to win the game 2–1. That Monday I was named first star. I'd skated to a familiar mix of boos and cheers from the crowd and kept rolling from there, scoring three goals through my first six games of the season.

Randy Carlyle was an old-school guy, but I seemed to thrive under his coaching; in fact, I think he was a big reason for my early success. He was a great communicator with his players. Randy would explain every decision that affected you. If you didn't get the minutes you wanted, he'd sit down and talk you through it himself instead of sending an assistant coach or just ignoring you completely. Randy never beat around the bush.

He also allowed his teams to move forward—he didn't dwell on the past. Instead of skating us after a terrible performance, for instance, he'd have us do a light scrimmage where we had to shoot from our unnatural side.

Before Randy took over I'd never gotten the impression that I was wanted in the lineup. And every time I did get minutes, the coaches didn't seem to think I deserved them. It was completely different with Randy. He made me feel not only that I belonged, but that I was a key part of the team's vision for success. For three years I'd been shat on for showing too much belief in myself. It turned out that all I needed was for others to believe in me too.

But Randy wasn't soft. If I messed up, he let me know. I respected that. And I was critical of myself, too. I just needed the chance to stick with the team through the ups and downs any player goes through in the season.

I played mostly on the third line alongside Clarke MacArthur and Leo Komarov. But Randy liked to mix things up. He knew I played a physical but skilled game and that I liked to get under people's skin. So he threw me out on the ice a few times alongside Colton Orr and Frazer McLaren, two absolute heavyweights. I looked up to both of these guys. They were veterans, tough as nails. By this point I'd watched Orrsie take on about six people.

When we first found out we were playing together, Orrsie sat next to me in the locker room and let me know how things were going to go.

"Listen man," he said. "You go out there and you do whatever the fuck you want. Nobody's going to come near you. Nobody will touch you. You run your mouth. You sucker-punch anybody. Nobody is going to do anything about it."

This was a big moment in our relationship, because Orrsie was an absolute prick when I first met him. He was a scary fucker, too. I didn't get intimated by many people, but Orrsie scared the living piss out of me.

It didn't help that I was a bit of a space cadet at the time. I didn't really get what playing in the NHL was like. I didn't know there was an unspoken rule book, and certainly didn't know how to treat veterans.

I'd be front row watching him make vicious knockouts against some of the league's toughest heavyweights—and we're talking real heavyweights. Nothing like it is now. I'd always sat beside him in the dressing room. I'd look over as he was tying his skates. His hands were enormous and none of his fingers were straight. They were all crooked. His hands were an absolute debacle, like he'd broken every little bone in them multiple times. I knew I never wanted to be on the receiving end of his fists. Orrsie also used to go the bathroom and cover his face in Vaseline before each game. I sat there thinking, "What the fuck is he doing?" One day I worked up the courage to ask him.

"What's with the Vaseline?" I said. "You're about to play a hockey game."

"Have you ever seen a boxer?" he asked me.

"Yeah."

"Well, when I get hit, the punches just slide off my face."

It was good advice. It's not going to do much if you get rocked. But apparently if you catch a slider of punch, it'll just glide off your face. I've never had to use that advice, but it was good to know.

In terms of tough guys, he was the real deal. He was ready to fight every single night. He took care of the team on the ice.

Orrsie was a guy who straightened me out whenever I did something to piss him off. Sometimes he was a little excessive. We used to play poker on the plane. One time, we played a round with a big pot. I was still young and was new to the team poker table. I thought everything was cool. We were just teammates playing for cash. I had an okay hand, but stayed in for the fun of it. I knew that I was probably going to lose. But then I hit something on the river and beat him. Orrsie absolutely lost it on me.

"This fucking kid . . ." he shouted. "Coming in . . ."

I can't remember what else he said, but he absolutely blasted me. Holy shit, I was petrified. We were on a fucking plane. Where was I going to hide?

"I'm sorry man," I said. "I didn't know it was that serious."

Wrong thing to say, Naz.

It was that serious. Orrsie wanted to slaughter me. And I had no allies, 30,000 feet up. Everyone was yelling at me at this point. As a rookie, I was getting harassed every single day. Winning a big poker hand just made it worse.

I survived that flight, but learned a valuable lesson.

"Oh man," I thought. "This is uncomfortable."

I didn't want it to happen again. So from that point on, I always lost at poker. I'd have a killer hand—pocket aces, full house, whatever. It didn't matter. If I beat Orrsie again, I knew he might murder me.

"Fold."

I folded so many hands to save my life. He doesn't even know how much money I could have taken from him.

As time went on, Orr became one of my favourite guys. I realized that he was showing me the way. He was making sure I paid my dues and learned to respect the league and my teammates. I came to have so much respect for him as a player and as a person.

Orr was the kind of teammate who protected his guys and put himself in harm's way so they could play their best. At first I kind of laughed when he told me I was safe beside him. But then I started thinking about it. It was true. Nobody would touch me while I was on the ice with Orr and McLaren.

Orr not only knew I was a bit of a target on the ice, he also knew I thrived when I could be a bit of an agitator. I liked being the kind of guy opponents hated, and Orr knew how effective that could be. And with Orr and McLaren beside me, I could indeed do whatever the hell I wanted—they were like my bodyguards. It was no-nonsense when we were together. I felt as if we were the Hanson brothers.

In February I was the team's leading scorer, with fourteen points in seventeen games. We'd won six of our last seven games heading into Tampa Bay, playing them the night after a win in Florida. But we were putting up a listless effort that night against the Lightning, trailing 4–1 with eight minutes to go in the third period. I was known mostly for my offensive ability at the time, but again, I also liked to play a physical game. I prided myself on being as effective on the first-line centre as I was on the checking line.

During a possession in the Lightning zone, Victor Hedman cross-checked me in the back at the left faceoff dot. It was a cheap shot—and I had a short fuse that day. So after we'd exchanged a few words as I got back up, I took a swipe at his stick. Hedman slashed me in the shin. It set me off. Fuck that. He'd initiated it and I had to stand up for myself. Plus, our team needed a jolt and I had nothing to lose.

So I cross-checked Hedman in the chest, which I kind of had to jump upward to do, because the guy is six-foot-six. Hedman went right at me. Instantly Orr was on top of him and then everyone on the ice swarmed together, tugging and pulling. I punched Hedman with my right. He fired back with a left. We both got in about four or five more shots in those few seconds before the linesmen were on us. It wasn't much of a tilt, but it would go down as my first NHL fight.

It was an important statement for me. Hedman, the second overall pick in my draft year, was a star defenceman. I didn't give a fuck.

A few games later I scored my first NHL hat trick in a 5–4 overtime win over the Islanders. The first two goals, in the first and second period, were wrist shots that fooled Evgeni Nabokov. The hatty came last in the second, when I deked past Ľubomír Višňovský and snapped the puck low on Nabokov's stick side. It was an incredible feeling, and made even better by the fact that we won by a single goal.

I'd finally reached the level that I'd told everyone I could, and that so many had declared I wouldn't. More importantly, it was helping the team. For the first time since I'd joined the franchise, it felt like we believed we could accomplish something special.

But after I added another two points a few nights later against the New Jersey Devils—where my old Rangers coach Pete DeBoer had landed—Carlyle was quick to temper the media attention I'd begun to receive. When reporters flooded him with questions about my play and how I'd been managed through the past few years, Carlyle responded with "You guys just want to anoint him, don't you?"

AS THE SEASON WOUND DOWN we were close to securing the Leafs' first playoff spot in nine seasons. And as we continued to find relative success on the ice, the energy and hype around the team built back up in our city.

And not just in Toronto. When we visited the Ottawa Senators in late March, I looked around Scotiabank Place—as the Sens' rink in Kanata was then called—and saw mostly blue and white jerseys. It was the coolest feeling. Our fans had turned a matchup in Ottawa into a home game.

It's one of the special things about playing for the Leafs that almost no other team experiences. As I mentioned earlier, it seems that wherever you go, your fans go—and especially in games within driving distance of Toronto's massive GTA. Games in Buffalo, Detroit, Ottawa, and even Montreal always had a huge audience of Leafs supporters.

It was incredible. That night, whenever we scored on the Senators in their own building, the entire place would erupt.

And playing alongside Joffrey Lupul and Nik Kulemin, who'd been moved to my line amid more shakeups, I made the Senators' building shake three times. The second hat trick of my career happened in that Ottawa rink full of Leafs fans. Each time we scored the whole stadium went nuts. I assisted on a goal from Lupul to get us on the board in the first period. Then I scored in the second and twice in the third—three straight for the natural—each assisted by Lupul. We both finished with four points.

After our 4–0 win, Don Cherry rushed into our locker room and dragged me into the nearby *Hockey Night in Canada* set. As my biggest media support from the very start, I was genuinely grateful to him for having my back through all the hard times. It was a wild moment in my career. And suddenly I was sitting on set between Ron MacLean and Cherry, with a white *Hockey Night in Canada* jersey on.

I'd watched this *Coach's Corner* segment every weekend growing up, but I'd never seen anyone on it who looked like me or had the same culture or faith. But there I sat, with Ron and Don, having scored my second NHL hat trick. It was surreal to think that now it was my face and my story being broadcast into homes across the country.

"It's been awesome, especially when things weren't going too well," I told MacLean. "You were the guy who picked me up out of the gutter . . . Things weren't going too well for a long time there. Grapes had my back from day one and I didn't want to let him down."

A few moments later Orr and McLaren joined us on set, at Cherry's insistence. They looked like they'd just gone through a war. McLaren bore the signs of a recent tilt. It was great to have my Hanson brothers join me on that stage. Like big brothers, they'd protected me until I found my confidence in the grit of our game. Before heading to a commercial break, Cherry noted that the scene was a lot like the time he'd pulled Leafs legend Doug Gilmour on set and famously gave him a kiss on the cheek.

"What does that mean? Are you going to kiss Nazem now?" MacLean asked.

Don gave me a big kiss on the cheek.

Looking back, if there was ever a time when I finally found my place with the Leafs and established myself in the NHL, it was that evening in Ottawa.

OVER THE NEXT MONTH AND the final dozen games, we finally secured our playoff appearance. I'd finish the season second in team scoring behind Kessel, with eighteen goals and twenty-six assists, playing the entire shortened season with the Leafs. There were no more questions about whether I belonged. I'd found my place in the NHL.

Our fifth-place finish in the Eastern Conference put us up against the Boston Bruins in the first round. It would be my first taste of playoff hockey in the show.

Heading to Boston in April 2013, it felt like nothing could go wrong.

12
"A VERY WINNABLE SERIES"

EVEN THOUGH WE'D FINISHED ONLY a few points behind the Bruins in the standings, we were widely considered the underdogs against Boston. A season earlier the Bruins had repeatedly kicked our ass, winning all six times we played against each other. They'd also won three of four meetings through the lockout season heading into the playoffs. The Bruins were a solid team, about to enter what would be an incredible era for the franchise. They were led upfront by Patrice Bergeron, Brad Marchand, and David Krejčí. Boston also had Zdeno Chára and Milan Lucic, adding some strength to their lineup. They even had the immortal Jaromir Jágr for a little ageless magic.

But we didn't really care about any of that. Playoff hockey is a lot different than the regular season—and the past doesn't mean shit.

We knew it would be a physical series, and that we'd need our offence to click if we were going to get through Boston. We didn't see ourselves as underdogs, though. There was a confidence about this group that hadn't existed before. We'd been a pretty good team through the regular season. And when it came to muscle, we could stand up to anyone in the league. We certainly weren't going to be intimidated by whoever the Bruins threw at us out there.

"This is a very, very winnable series for us," I told reporters at the morning skate before the first game in Boston.

Still, I had the predictable jitters ahead of my first playoff game. I was both excited and nervous. But when we got on the ice at TD Garden to the rabid jeering of the Bruins fans, I felt that familiar rush of adrenalin. I loved this stuff. I was always as hyped to play in an opposing team's barn as I was in our own. It's a different vibe, sure. In one you're the hero, the other you're the villain. Both roles are ridiculously fun to play.

We scored in the first two minutes of the first, but then played like a team that hadn't been in a playoff series for nearly a decade. We seemed nervous out there, giving up way too many turnovers as the Bruins pushed us around. The speed and intensity of NHL play-off hockey had kicked up a notch from what I was used to. I loved that, but it would take an adjustment. Boston outgunned us in pretty much every area. They doubled our shot count with forty fired on Reimer to the twenty we managed to direct at Rask. We lost 4–1.

I didn't play great, which really grated on me. The Bruins were a veteran squad and had been through this kind of intensity before. I felt out of place, and it pissed me off. Some reporters pontificated on how I looked like a junior player on the ice, literally out of my league. I couldn't blame them. I had several stupid turnovers and was caught flat-footed too many times. As I've said before, although those who didn't know me had the notion that I was arrogant, I was much harder on myself than they could ever be. Throughout our practice the next day at Boston University, I carried my poor performance like an anvil. I couldn't wait to get back on the ice to put that first disappointing playoff appearance behind me.

In our next outing, I found my game. During the second period Carlyle switched up our lines and put me alongside Kessel and Ryan Hamilton. Then, off a blocked Bruins shot less than a minute into the period, I fired a pass up the middle to Kessel, who broke in on a breakaway and went five-hole on Rask. It was a huge moment for Phil, who'd been harassed by Chára in both games—as well as by the seventeen thousand fans who were all over him. He hadn't scored an even-strength goal against his old team in twenty-four games. It was the spark we needed. We played like the team we knew we were—a team that wouldn't be pushed around and would take advantage of any mistakes the other side made.

Kessel's goal stood up as the winner. We left Boston with a 4–2 win, happy to have split the first two games of the series away.

THE LEADUP TO GAME 3 in Toronto was one of the most enjoyable things I'd ever experienced. You could feel the pent-up excitement surrounding our first home playoff game in nine long seasons. Fans were everywhere; the entire city seemed to be dressed in blue and white. Leafs flags waved outside car windows. Every restaurant and bar was packed; it was as if the whole city had shut down to celebrate our home game. And Maple Leaf Square—the area just outside the Air Canada Centre, where fans would gather to watch our games—was introduced for the first time. Raptors fans would later adopt the idea with their Jurassic Park, which became famous in its own right. At the time it marked a new era, and now it's a tradition.

Inside, the national anthem thundered as though we were about to go to war. The energy was incredible. But that kind of energy doesn't always translate into success, especially when the other team's goalie gets hot. We fired forty-seven shots on Rask in Game 3, which was the most shots we'd had in a game that season, but he turned aside all but two. We lost 5–2.

Despite the disappointment, the crowd sustained its intensity through our second match at home. It was a thrilling back-and-forth game.

In the third period I picked up four minutes for high-sticking after my blade clipped Chris Kelly and drew blood. Watching from the penalty box, those four minutes felt like an hour. But as I sat in the box, feeling the weight of the series crushing down on me, Reimer made two huge glove saves to keep the game tied at three.

I exhaled. We held on till the end of regulation.

Two minutes into overtime I had a chance in tight on the net, but Rask reached across to rob me right on the doorstep. I was that close to scoring my first playoff goal and sending us back to Boston with the series tied at two. But it wasn't meant to be. With just under seven minutes to go in the first, Krejčí scored his third of the game on a two-on-one rush, beating Reimer with a shot that clipped him under his arm and rolled over the goal line.

It was a cruel ending to a rip-roaring game. But it was also what playoffs are all about.

Losing both games at home was tough, a demoralizing blow after feeling so much energy in our own rink. And now, heading back to Boston down three games to one, Game 5 would be the biggest test of our collective resilience we'd faced. Everything was on the line. As a young player, I'd never encountered this kind of tension in the show before. Meanwhile veterans like Phaneuf and Kessel didn't seem fazed. It was all business with them, especially when they were on the ropes.

At that Game 5, Bruins fans seemed ready to celebrate and advance to the next round. Carlyle moved me to the top six to shake things up. After playing mostly on the third line all season, I was now going to centre our top two lines—meaning everyone would be looking to me to step up and have a big night. Our season was riding on it. I felt an immense amount of pressure, but I embraced it. I was ready for the moment.

I also felt better about my game than I had at the start of the series.

In the final period, the Bruins did everything they could to eliminate us. It was a complete onslaught. They outshot us nineteen to four—and we blocked twenty shots. It was a statement game for us. Even though we were on the edge of being eliminated, we weren't about to fall apart. Reimer stood on his head. He was incredible, making forty-four saves in the game. The Bruins had one last chance to tie it with four seconds to play. Again, Reimer turned the puck aside.

We survived, bruised and battered. Now we just had to head home and survive again. There's nothing in sports more gruelling, thrilling, and pressure packed than NHL playoff hockey.

Somehow we gutted out back-to-back 2–1 wins, with Reimer still standing in his head to keep us alive.

Having played in a Memorial Cup final, I thought I knew a lot about playoff hockey. But in those six games of my first NHL playoff series, I'd been put through a master class. Collectively, we'd held together when it looked as if we didn't have a hope in hell. Personally, I'd been up and down, trying to find my game when the pressure reached its highest point. I'd made mistakes, but I'd also played a key part in keeping us in the series.

Taking those two games back to back was an incredible rush. But there wasn't time to congratulate ourselves. A scheduling conflict meant we had to play Game 7 less than twenty-four hours later in Boston, so after the win our bus drove straight to the airport and we hopped on our charter to New England.

Coming off that pair of wins, we had all the momentum. This series had belonged to Boston, but we'd refused to hand it to them. We'd survived two elimination games. Our confidence had swung from dejection to belief. We were right back in it; the Bruins were the ones on the ropes now. Still, we refused to get ahead of ourselves. We knew it was a tough building to go into on the road. We knew it was going to be a difficult task. We knew Boston was the type of team that would scratch and claw to the end.

AFTER THE PUCK DROPPED AT Boston Garden for Game 7, everything seemed to go in our favour. The hockey gods are cruel that way. Cody Franson scored twice, in the first and second periods, to give us a 2–1 lead heading into the third. Then, a couple minutes into the final period, Kessel scored off a rebound from a shot by James van Riemsdyk that Rask had bobbled.

3–1.

We were right there, on the edge.

A few minutes later I rushed in on a two-on-one with Kessel. He fired a perfect shot off Rask's right pad as I drove to the net. The puck skidded into my path and I slapped it into the open net as Rask dove in vain.

Finally. I turned to Kessel and shouted. It was my first playoff goal, and it couldn't have come at a sweeter time. It'd been an intense atmosphere all game. Now the Garden was dead silent. The Bruins bench looked defeated; they hung their heads in shock. We were up 4–1 with fifteen minutes left to play. And that three-goal gap was a big leap from being up by two. With a two-goal lead Bruins fans could still hope. Down three? Even the most obnoxious among them would have admitted it was pretty much over.

Back in Toronto, twenty thousand fans gathered at the Air Canada Centre and in Maple Leaf Square, getting ready to celebrate our move to the second round.

The atmosphere was unmistakable: some kind of Leafs history was about to be made. We felt pretty damn good.

For the next six minutes the Bruins played as though time was ticking away on their hope. Reimer stood tall. We had them.

Then, with just over ten minutes to go, Lucic barrelled through our zone and around the goal like a freight train, tossing a pass in front that somehow found Nathan Horton in the slot. Reimer tried to slide across with his right pad and blocker, but it was too late.

The Garden jolted up as if it had just received a shot from a defibrillator.

Lucic roared at his bench, a living jab of adrenalin.

Shit. Okay, don't panic. Just ten minutes to go.

We held on to that two-goal lead well into relatively safe territory. And knowing we couldn't let up, we kept Boston's desperate attempts at bay until they were forced to pull Rask for an extra man with less than two minutes to go.

The Bruins were relentless. Lucic connected with a hard check on Carl Gunnarsson in our corner to keep possession. He shovelled the puck to Horton behind our net, who passed it back to Chára on the blue line. He quickly fired a low shot at Reimer, who kicked it aside. But Krejčí regained possession and cycled it to Patrice Bergeron on the point, who fed it back to the giant. Chára one-timed another shot. This time the rebound bounced in directly in front of Reimer. And Lucic, who'd started the attack with his hit on Gunnarsson, was right there to tap the puck into our net.

The Garden gasped with life.

One minute, twenty-two seconds to go. Do Not Blow This.

All the confidence we'd held before was gone. In a flash, it was 4–3 and we had a minute—an eternity—left to play. The building was absolutely on fire. My mind was bouncing all over the place. We were battling all the elements. Respect to Boston: they are a tough crowd.

Now we were just holding on to survive.

The Bruins attacked. With less than a minute to go Lucic won another puck behind our net, retaining Boston possession. He moved it back and forth across from the point to the boards as Chára set up a wall in front of Reimer. *Jágr to Bergeron . . . Bergeron to Krejčí . . . Krejčí to Bergeron . . .*

Bergeron, dead centre at the point. He fired the puck through a crowd toward the net.

The beast rose in the Garden and lunged to devour us.

4–4.

Holy fucking shit.

To this day I've never heard a building so rowdy or so loud, and I've played in some big games with some wild crowds.

But this was something else entirely. I thought the roof was going to collapse. That's not an exaggeration. The building shook. Pieces of debris were falling from the ceiling. Literally. You could literally see pieces falling to the ice.

Holy shit. This is absolutely insane. We could be in trouble here.

The third ended. Intermission. We all filed into the locker room before sudden-death overtime. We'd been on the verge of completing one of the most dramatic stories in Toronto sports history. What the hell just happened? As a young player, I was like a deer in the headlights. I'd played in big games: the OHL championship, the Memorial

Cup, a gold medal match, the Calder Cup final. But this was a whole different level.

Is it always this nuts? This is absolute bananas.

Everyone was stunned as we sat through intermission. Absolutely stunned.

Some of the veteran guys in the dressing room broke the silence. I remember Dion and Phil doing most of the talking. The message was clear: If at the beginning of this series we'd said we'd be one goal away from advancing, we probably would have accepted it. Now we just had to finish the job.

That was the mentality we had. It was the only one we could take. But it's easier said than done, especially when you emerge from the dressing room and the building is still shaking. As we returned to the ice, the Garden seemed just as loud as before, the fans relentless. The Bruins had all the momentum on their side, and they knew it.

Six minutes into overtime, after a flurry of Boston shots, Brad Marchand snuck in from the right side of the slot and tapped in a rebound.

And just like that, we were done.

The building might have collapsed and I couldn't have cared.

I DIDN'T GET MUCH SLEEP that night. It took a couple of days to process. It wasn't until we returned to Toronto to clear out our lockers and I said goodbye to everyone as they headed out for the off-season that the realization began to truly set in.

That's when you understand. Because no one is ever *expecting* to go home. You're going in there every day expecting to win, expecting to move on. You're showing up at the rink, attending meetings, putting so much time and preparation into the game, and all in the hope that you'll advance. But when you lose Game 7, it's over. And then suddenly, in a blink, you're packing your bags, you're clearing out your condo, you're booking tickets back home.

It's a brutal disappointment. To this day, losing that series was one of the toughest feelings I've ever experienced. To be so close and then to have it taken away so fast.

Is this what NHL playoff hockey is like?

It made me appreciate just what it takes to be in the playoffs. Through the grind of the series, I came to understand the magnitude, the pressure, the intensity of the post-season.

But I was still naive.

Back then, I figured this was just the beginning.

I knew, of course, that the older guys, coming to the end of their careers, wouldn't have the same luxury of time. But I was still too young to really appreciate how that might feel. For me, the disappointment lasted through the summer. But as a young guy, I didn't understand how much worse the veterans must have felt at that time.

Hopefully we're going to be in this situation a lot. I believed we could have easily been on the other side of the overtime winner.

There was still so much to learn. It was the kind of lesson that resonates more with each passing year. It became part of my mentality as a player. And although it evolved with time, the sting of that loss never fully healed. I won't let myself forget.

What was true in the dressing room before overtime is always true. The better you do, the higher the stakes. The closer you get to greatness, the more you risk being crushed. Would we have been better off getting swept by the Bruins? Losing in 6? The fact is, that loss stung so much because we came so close to upsetting a very good hockey team. It's always that way. That's why a Game 7 is different from the pre-season. You care more. You care a lot. And when you care, you risk getting burned. The more you have to gain, the more

you have to lose. What good teams and good players have to learn—
what we all have to learn—is that you have to *really* want success
to be willing to risk the devastation of disappointment. Trust me,
the cost is high. I learned the hard way.

13

AN OPPORTUNITY MY GRANDFATHER NEVER HAD

WHEN YOU NEGOTIATE A CONTRACT in the NHL, everyone knows your business—or at least they think they know your business.

The loss to the Bruins stung throughout that 2013 off-season, but there was some small consolation in that the lockout year had been my best season as a Leaf. I'd finally been able to prove my value to the club, vindication for the lack of faith I felt the team had had in me through the previous few years.

I was at the end of my entry-level contract, which made me a restricted free agent that summer. This meant the Leafs owned my rights, so I was basically at their mercy. On the other hand, I was twenty-two years old and playing the best hockey of my life. I'd made just over $1.7 million a year through my first four years as a Leaf, with performance bonuses, which I was incredibly grateful for. I'd never take for granted how fortunate I was to make the kind of money I did as an NHL player.

But now I could put a value on what I believed I was worth in the NHL market. It was an exciting time, but also a frustrating one. And my first experience negotiating a contract in Toronto proved to be a bit of a grind.

Even though discussions between my agent and the team were done in confidence, everyone seemed to believe they knew what I was asking for and had opinions on what I was worth. There was speculation all summer long that I was asking for a ridiculous amount of money, which just wasn't true.

It's funny how narratives can get established. Half the articles written and comments made on the radio that summer were full of shit. None of it was true. I don't know who was pumping it out there, but the story was always that I was an overconfident kid asking for an unprecedented contract, when all my agent and I wanted was something fair and in line with what comparable players had already received. There was nothing greedy or unexpected about our ask. But I was made out to be a bad apple who put myself before the team.

This was a new world for me. I was used to being criticized as a player, to being told I was overconfident and so on. As I've said, that nonsense only fuelled me. But for it to be implied that I was greedy and selfish was frustrating because there was no way to defend myself. These were private negotiations that seemed to be aired publicly—with only one side presented.

Anyone in the same situation would want to get the best deal possible. It's business. It's a negotiation. And a fair one. Still, it bothered me that everyone seemed to believe what they heard or read about me. It was all speculation. And when that speculation is mistaken for the truth, it can be maddening. How can you know the truth when you're completely misinformed?

But that happened a lot in Toronto. The media sets a certain narrative and fans buy into it. Whether it's true or not, it's just something for them to talk about, part of the entertainment. With time I'd come to understand that. I'd learn to live with it, as all players must. But as a young guy, it ate away at me.

I tried my best to steer clear of all the garbage out there. But my contract negotiations were big news that summer, so it was hard to stay away. I was living in Toronto full time by then, and it seemed that no matter what I did, it was impossible to escape. Meanwhile negotiations continued through those summer months, this time with Dave Nonis, who'd replaced Brian Burke the previous January.

The Leafs knew I was stuck unless I was willing to sit it out, and so they tried to convey that they'd easily move on without me. I've already talked about how unclear they'd been about whether I had any value to them. I'd never known where I sat on the team's depth chart, and my extended stints in the minors—not to mention that movie recommendation I was given—made the team's vision for me seem ambiguous. But I was confident enough to know what I could bring to a team and to know what I was worth. This was my career. This contract was incredibly important to me and my future. I was going to take my time and get it right.

The facts weren't very complicated. The Leafs made an offer, and I was looking for something different. They had the upper hand. I had very little leverage.

As training camp neared there was side speculation that I was planning to hold out. That part was true. I was preparing myself for having to put some pressure on the organization by missing camp.

And I knew my teammates would understand, since everyone in that locker room faces the same reality at some point. We know what the situation is. On the outside, there's so much talk about players being greedy and not putting their teammates first. But we all get it, and we all want each other to do as well as possible in contract negotiations.

In the end, I knew that holding out through training camp wasn't something I really wanted to do. I wanted to prepare and get ready for the season. Nor did the team want me to sit out. I'd proven that I was a valuable part of the club.

Our contract discussions dragged on much longer than I'd wanted, and probably could have concluded sooner. It was all a huge distraction at a time when I'd much rather have put all my focus on the team and the upcoming season. And so, just before training camp began, we figured something out. I showed up on the first day of camp having agreed to a two-year deal worth $5.8 million.

I was happy with the outcome. It was fair for both sides, and I was relieved to have that conversation behind me. Not only was it friendly to the team's cap restraints, but the bridge deal also set me up to show everyone what I was worth when I'd enter unrestricted free agency as a twenty-five-year-old.

The experience was eye-opening, though. I saw firsthand how misinformation can be reported as fact and how that can impact the way people perceive you. It was a frustrating reality, but it was something I had to learn to live with. And it wouldn't be the last time.

AFTER FINALLY SIGNING THAT CONTRACT, my first thought was of my grandfather. The OG had been in poor health for several years. He suffered from diabetes, his hands were stiff with painful arthritis, he had high blood pressure, and he'd recently experienced a collapsed lung. But my grandfather had endured so much in his life that he pushed through old age as though it was just another test of his indomitable will.

Because of his health, he was unable to attend many of my games in Toronto. And yet, even though he was no longer standing at the glass in the corner while I played, I knew he was always watching. He never missed a game. We spoke several times a week, talking about a sport he'd known nothing about when he first arrived in Canada.

The architect of my dreams never touched the ice, but he made the impossible a reality by giving up everything for the betterment of his family.

As a child, my grandfather lived in the southern part of Lebanon, in a village called Kfar Danis, close to the Syrian border. The "El Kadri" family is one of many who were well known in the region. Today the village is even more remote than when my grandfather lived there. Many people have left, most of them migrating to new countries.

When he was four years old my grandfather's parents died, suffering strokes within months of each other, leaving him an orphan. He was raised by his grandparents. Growing up, he didn't have much in the way of formal schooling, but he learned how to read and write Arabic on his own. Before his tenth birthday he was working as a farmhand for a nearby fruit grower.

In 1968, when he was in his early thirties, my grandfather left Lebanon for Canada with no way of knowing what possibilities lay ahead. At first he lived in Windsor, Ontario, where he had some relatives. But a short time later he moved his family two hours down the road to London.

He didn't speak a word of English when he arrived and knew very little over the next forty-five years. Instead he got by on his work ethic, taking low-paying factory jobs, cleaning the bowling alley in the evenings. He grinded out those greater opportunities from the circumstances he'd been given.

My grandfather taught me to fight for what I want in life. He taught me determination. When you want something, go out and work hard enough to get it.

He was so excited when I was drafted by the Leafs. Despite knowing nothing about hockey he was always in my corner, banging the glass. Whenever I was sent to the penalty box, he'd call it "habbis," the Lebanese word for "jail." And he was there, in Montreal, the day I was drafted, that unimaginable future coming into view because of him. He and my grandmother, Sharfi, would go on to have twenty-one grandchildren. And my siblings, my cousins—in all their successes and the love they share with the families they build—we all rise from the foundation they laid.

When I signed that contract with the Leafs in September 2013, I called my grandfather about my plan to travel with him to Beirut. It was a plan I'd had for years. Although I'd made good money through my initial contract, negotiating my first significant pay bump seemed the perfect time to finally make those plans a reality. I'd never been to Lebanon, the land that cradled my proud heritage. I wanted to learn more about where my story began. And I wanted my grandfather to tell me all about it, and for him to experience the rare joy of returning to the start of his journey at least one last time. He seemed enthusiastic about the prospect; he wanted to show me everything.

When we spoke in early December, I didn't know how significant that call would be. At the time it was just another part of the weekly routine we had, one of several chats I'd have with him as he rested back in London.

By then my grandfather had been in and out of the hospital for several weeks and was living with my uncle, Hiseam, while receiving care. He was weak, but our conversations seemed to breathe life into him. And he always seemed to be doing better after we played. I don't know why, but I think he just loved knowing that I was living my dream.

That Sunday evening, we talked about the San Jose Sharks. The Leafs would be playing them in a few days, and so we chatted about how the team might do against the powerhouse squad, who were still among the favourites to win the Cup. My grandfather said he was looking forward to watching us play.

As we hung up that night, I didn't know it was the last time we'd say goodbye. But that's how most endings work. There's seldom time to say thank you in the way you'd want.

He was supposed to go for a doctor's appointment the next morning. My aunt arrived to pick him at seven a.m. and found him unconscious. I'd just woken up and was getting ready to leave for practice when I got the call.

I left for London shortly after learning the news. It's a Muslim custom to bury the dead within a day.

It was very sad for us as we gathered to mourn the man who'd given us hope and taught us to believe in ourselves. I'd never experienced that kind of absence before. Everyone I'd loved in my life was always there. It was particularly difficult to see my father lose *his* father. I saw Dad's enormous heart break. It's one of those moments that stick with you.

When he was young, my father, who never got to play organized hockey, would walk several kilometres from their house in the middle of winter, through the piercing wind, to play hockey on a frozen pond. He'd learned the spirit of determination and tenacity from his father and passed it on to me—changing the course of that spirit's inherent possibility.

It makes you grateful for people in your life, and more aware that one day, far too soon, they'll be gone. That's life. It's a wonderful gift, but it's hard sometimes. I've learned that it's important not to lose sight of the people and things that matter most—and to enjoy every day while working hard for every opportunity we're given.

It was difficult to think that my grandfather would no longer be watching. I thought about the trip we never took together, and of all the great moments to come that we wouldn't be able to share. I'd envisioned one day raising the Stanley Cup above my head—another height reached in the dream he'd left us to complete. I'd hoped he'd be there to see that dream come true. But now I knew that it didn't matter much. His dream already had.

I returned to the Leafs the day after my grandfather was buried. It hurt like hell. But we were in the middle of a five-game losing streak, and there was work to do. I kept my grandfather's example close to my heart: to fight through adversity. It was the best tribute I could give him. The original Nazem Kadri wouldn't have wanted it any other way.

14
AFTERMATH

THAT SEASON—MY FIRST FULL, EIGHTY-TWO-GAME season—I set a career high with twenty goals and fifty points. I finished third in team scoring behind Phil Kessel and James van Riemsdyk, and continued being an important presence down the middle. It felt like I'd finally arrived with the Leafs in a meaningful way. I was crossing an important threshold in my career, establishing myself as the player I'd believed I could be.

I wasn't handed it on a silver spoon, that's for sure. I had to work hard and make my way through a lot of bullshit to get it—and then once I did, I started the season hot and ended up being one of our best players that year.

But there were still a lot of lessons to be learned. The collapse against Boston the previous spring lingered all season long. It was inescapable. It still is, really. It's one of those things that has come back again and again, whether it's through highlight shows or commentators dredging up the past. When you blow it in such spectacular fashion, you kind of earn your place in infamy.

In hindsight, though, that loss was one of the most important experiences of my career. At the time, you don't know what you're going through; it's just so raw. But reflecting on it now, I can see how valuable that series against Boston was in shaping my perspective as a player.

You need to have that turn-the-page mentality, even though it's hard to manage in the moment.

I still think about that series and how close we were—and how shitty it was. If we could have just borne down or caught a break everything could have been different. Who knows how far we might have advanced? Boston went on to the Stanley Cup finals. You can't help thinking *That could have been us.* I think we were good enough to have made that kind of push. We had the momentum that year to be one of the last teams standing.

You're always a bit salty about that kind of stuff, but in sports you have no choice but to regroup. I learned a lot from those veteran guys. That's sports. You're going to face difficulty, and ninety-nine percent of the time, you're going to fail, but you're always chasing that one percent.

THE COLLAPSE CAME INTO A fuller light in 2014 as we missed the playoffs in a late-season tailspin. We'd been in a playoff position most of the season, but then we went 2–12 through its final fourteen games.

At the time, you kind of don't realize the magnitude of that loss. As I said earlier, when you don't make the playoffs as a young player, you just think, *Okay, we'll have another shot. Maybe next year, maybe the year after that.* I just assumed I'd get another chance.

And yet, once you do make the playoffs, any team has the potential to win. In my opinion, it's the best league in the world for that reason. With the parity in the NHL, any team can achieve success at any given moment. It's not like the NBA or the Premier League where you have maybe three powerhouse teams, and one of those teams usually wins it. But it goes the other way, too. A lot can change in the span of six months or a year. You can go from being one of the best teams in the league to not even making the next season's playoffs.

So when you start gaining more experience, you learn that when you are able to advance, you've got to bear down. Complacency is a huge mistake. It'll kill you. That's the NHL. When you have a shot at finishing off an opponent, you've got to take it—you have to be ruthless enough to make sure they can't claw their way back in. The players will be just too good to do otherwise. It's survival of the fittest. Give any team in the league a sliver of hope and they'll run with it.

In other words, you learn not to take things for granted. Be present. Don't look past the moment.

This all might sound obvious, but these were important lessons for me. Failure helps form your character. And as I got older, the mistakes I made ended up shaping my approach to the game.

It's funny. When you are in high school, four years feels like forever. Every minute counts when you are still growing and learning. And, yes, *developing*. For me, those years with the Leafs were kind of like that. I had some great times, but it was definitely not all fun. There was a lot of frustration, a lot of anger, a lot of disappointment. A *lot*. And it seemed to go on forever. But that's just what it feels like to learn. I didn't know what was down the road for me. I just knew I had to keep pushing to get there. Times like that make you who you are. I guess that is why I think so much about those early years. I am not especially interested in thinking about who I *am* today. It is probably not healthy to think about that. But remembering how you got here—especially how you learned from your mistakes—that is the best way to keep learning.

AT THAT TIME IN MY career, I was starting to show more maturity on the ice and absorbing some difficult lessons.

Randy Carlyle could be a hardass, just as Ron Wilson had been. He was straightforward and let you know exactly what he thought of how you were playing. Randy had no problem dropping me down to one of our checking lines to send a message. It happened quite a few times.

Getting bumped down sucks. There's no way around that. You want to play with the highly skilled guys.

It wasn't really a conversation, though, because I was a younger guy. As a veteran you get a little more respect in these situations. With younger guys you just kind of look at the board and you see where you are. You understand that you haven't been playing your best and that you might get bumped down. That's professional sports.

In most cases, I'd probably have a conversation with Randy on the ice after the morning skate. He'd say something along those lines of "Hey, get your ass going." It was direct and brutally honest, never sugar-coated. But I was always a guy who could take the heat.

Because, really, there are only two ways you can take that kind of thing. You can sit and sulk or you can go out there and show them they were wrong, that you're capable of playing your game on whatever line they stick you on. That's always the approach I've had. I've tried not to be too hard on myself. Whatever situation I'm in, I put my head down and go to work—and do whatever I have to do to play the way I need to play.

I won't pretend that it didn't bother me. It absolutely did. But there was no question in my mind that I'd get back up to where I'd been before. I knew I would get there.

It was just one of those phases where I had to find my stride and do whatever I could to get myself into the game—to go out and kind

Strange to say, I grew up a Habs fan, as you can see from this photo of my dad and me watching *Hockey Night in Canada* a long time ago. But even when I was just a tyke in House League back in London, I loved the game, no matter which crest was on the front of my sweater.

Junior hockey is a pretty intense few years. You're a regular high school kid, and playing hockey with and against the guys who are going to be the future of the league. I played with some great guys—and a great coach—in Kitchener, where we won the OHL championship. I was actually traded to my hometown London Knights *before* that, but didn't suit up for them until the following season. And despite some bad luck with injuries, I got a second crack at the World Juniors in 2010. Here I am putting the puck behind American goalie Jack Campbell in the shootout during the final game. Campbell ended up playing in Toronto too.

You are on top of the world when you hear your name in the NHL draft, especially when it's Brian Burke calling it. But you soon realize there is a long, long way to go before you can be a regular contributor. It took me a few training camps and some tough love from the Leafs' staff before I could claim my place on the team. But I never lost my confidence, and I had incredible support. As always, my family was there for me every step of the way. And the support of ultra-old school Don Cherry told me I was doing something right all along. The support of Colton Orr and Frazer McLaren didn't hurt either. With your family, Grapes, and those two on your side, you are going to be in good shape.

There is something special about playing in Toronto. Things didn't always go our way, and the media scrutiny was intense. But we had a special group of guys and some incredible talent. Here I am celebrating a Tyler Bozak goal with Mikhail Grabovski and Phil Kessel. And that's me at the bottom, soaking up the moment I scored my first hat trick in the show.

It would be easy to make the mistake of thinking that mine is a story about hockey. But no one's story is really about what they are lucky enough to do for a job. Everyone's deepest story is about family. I got a bit more time in the spotlight than most, but everything I did, I did for the generations that came before me and the generations that came after.

It felt weird wearing a sweater other than the Leafs' blue and white when Ashley and I moved to Denver. But we quickly realized it was a gift. We loved the city, and I got to play with some of the most talented players in the game (above, that's me with Cale Makar). Maybe even more than that, the fans in Colorado showed their true colours when I faced a storm of racism during the 2022 Playoffs. They were pure class.

Every player dreams of winning the Cup. When you finally get your hands on it, all the years you spent chasing it come flooding back. It is an incredible rush of emotion. Every player has his own unique path to that moment, but they all say pretty much the same thing if they are lucky enough to lift it: thanks. They all want to share it with the people who helped get them there. For me, that meant the mosque in London, Ontario, and it meant my family. Thank you.

Some things never change, like going to the rink with my dad. It has been an incredible journey from the outdoor ice in London to the Calgary Saddledome, and I know I wouldn't have gotten far without my family. In Calgary, I was named to the All-Star team for the second time. It was an honour to represent the Flames amongst the games' best players—and it was nice to catch up with my former teammates Cale Makar, Mikko Rantanen, and Nathan MacKinnon from that stacked Avalanche roster. That's Seth Jones over to my left.

of show that I belonged there. I wanted it to turn into a wake-up call for the staff, too. If I was playing alongside a guy like Colton Orr, I was going to play tough and make life a living hell for whoever we lined up against. I wanted the coaches to say "Holy shit, this guy is not soft."

The NHL is all about that. You have to earn that respect. You have to pay your dues and earn your stripes. And every once in a while you've got to show people that you're not going to get stepped on.

The public nature of those demotions also adds a layer of humiliation. It's tough in times like that because the fans know you've been demoted and you're going to get questions about it from reporters. And when you're feeling gloomy and pissed off, especially after a loss or a bad performance, it can be hard to have twenty cameras on you as you explain to everyone why you're on the fourth line. It's embarrassing. But part of the job requirement is to answer those tough questions. You have to stand up and be accountable.

Shortly after I was drafted, we had media training that taught us how to manage an interview and control the conversation. It was a little class they put on for the guys who'd just been drafted. Stand up tall, look bigger, don't let people hover around you—simple things that just make an interview come off better.

But the biggest things are mental. It is natural to feel obligated to answer any question that is thrown your way when you are being interviewed. It just seems polite. That's what normal people do in a conversation. But an interview only *looks like* a conversation. The reality is, just answering the questions is a terrible idea. Some interviewers want to know what you think, and some just want to get you to say what they want to hear. If you want to get across what you really mean, you learn to control the interview. You answer what you want to answer. The interviewer gets to ask the question. That's his or her job. But only you get to decide how you want to respond. Thinking about it that way makes a big difference.

I've always been a people person, so I'm usually pretty good at holding conversations and being respectful. Of course, there are many times when someone in the media is not as respectful. Some even have a reputation for that, and you kind of want to tell them to fuck off every once in a while. You do that with a little bit of attitude—but you have to do it politically, because you're surrounded by cameras and that stuff lives forever. But you get your point across, and maybe they ease up a little bit.

I was always relatively honest with myself—and with the media—about whether I played well or if I thought I played like shit. I don't think anyone was either asking or telling me anything I didn't already know.

Those are the moments when you grow the most. A hockey season—a hockey career—is all about facing failure. Everything changes from game to game. You're hot, then you're not. Your confidence wavers. Everything you think you know about the game is challenged. You start doubting yourself.

So it's important to stay on an even keel and not get too excited when you win a big game or too disappointed when you lose one. You have to remain level—it's just too exhausting to go up and down constantly over an eighty-two-game season and nine months of hockey. It can be a physical and mental rollercoaster, and you have to be prepared to ride it.

The game is about showing character in the midst of trouble. When things are going well, when you're scoring a couple points a night and you're filling the back of the net, it's easy to lace up and go out there in practice. But how do you act when things aren't going your way, when you haven't scored in ten or fifteen games and you're in a bit of a rut? That's when true character comes into play. And it's something you've got to prove to the staff, prove to your team-mates. It comes down to how you respond to failure—and in many ways, that's more important than constant success.

And I think a big reason why I've been as successful as I have is what I learned along the way from men like my grandfather and father. They faced all kinds of obstacles just trying to build a life for their families. Being criticized for playing a poor game is nothing compared to grinding out day and night to put food on the table in hopes of a better future. That reality has always helped keep things in perspective for me.

Something Martin Luther King Jr. once said really connected with me and has become a sort of mantra for my career. I revisit it often, whenever I need to be reminded that real growth comes amid the hardest difficulties: "The ultimate measure of a man is not where he stands in moments of convenience and comfort, but where he stands at times of challenge and controversy."

This doesn't mean pretending that the strains of life have no effect on you. It's okay to show your cracks. In fact, it's important. It makes you stronger.

THERE'S THIS GENERAL ASSUMPTION THAT because you're a professional hockey player, you should be able to take all kinds of pressure and criticism. That you should be "tough." But that's an attitude that I've seen evolve over the course of my career, which has straddled two very different generations.

When I started in the league there was a culture of trying to deter-mine a young player's toughness—a "Let's see what they're made of" kind of thing. But now we're much more aware of how damaging that kind of approach can be. A player's mental health has since become much more important. And professional athletes already have enough stress going on. We don't need to add any more unnecessarily.

Everyone is their own person. Everyone deals with issues their own way. Nowadays with the younger players going into the league, there's more sensitivity, and we have to respect that. The past decade has been a time of transition between an old-school and a new-school mentality.

I now have more of a new-school approach to the game. But in the past, coming up in that transition phase, I know I could rub people the wrong way.

Now you see a lot of new faces in coaching and management. The old boys club is starting to fracture as younger people come into those roles. Part of it is that the attitude toward success has shifted as well. Doing something because it's always been done that way is no longer a good enough rationale if it's not working. Innovation drives success. Fresh ideas, new perspectives—a more diverse way of thinking about the game is what's valued now.

I've had a lot of great coaches, but almost all came with a coaching philosophy that I'd consider old school. That's not to knock any of those men. They all had tremendous success coaching the way they did. After all, there are many different ways to find success as a coach.

Dale Hunter, with the Knights, was a much more mellow kind of guy. He could get fiery, but it was always a less-is-more kind of approach. He certainly didn't try to get in your head. It was all hockey with him.

Ron Wilson and Randy Carlyle were both very old-style NHL coaches. Those guys went about their business differently, but they had the same sort of foundation. They could be hardasses who demanded a lot. They could be pricks at times, but again they had some success with that.

Often coaches get stuck in a certain way of operating. If it's worked for them in the past, they stick with it. They don't adapt, and they end up trying to force their method onto players it doesn't work with. I get it—that's the foundation of their coaching. It's what they're used to and what they're comfortable with. But in dealing with certain people, you have to be able to switch it up—or not switch it up—depending on your personnel.

More than ever, there's a need for different management styles and different ways of leading a team. It's cultural. It's an age thing. It's generational. Times have changed, and there can often be a bit of a disconnect. If you're approaching some of your younger players in the same manner you've had for decades, it's not likely to translate or come across in the same way.

Players change, coaching changes, and it's important to adapt.

15
GREAT TEAMMATES, BAD TEAM

OVER THE COURSE OF A career, you'll inevitably connect with some teams more than others. That's a reality of pro sports. There are seasons when the roster just works, on and off the ice. When the group becomes more like a family than a collection of guys who get paid well to play a sport and try to win.

That's what I found in Toronto in the early 2010s. It's an era for the team that's always overlooked—dismissed, perhaps fairly, because of our lack of relative success on the ice. After losing that first-round series against the Bruins in 2013, it would take five seasons before we reached the playoffs again. So that particular Leafs era takes a bit of a beating—and this in the age of Dion Phaneuf and Phil Kessel, two great guys who deserved a lot more respect than they were given.

I get it. Toronto fans are passionate. We all want success—the ultimate measure of how a team is remembered. And by that standard, we didn't measure up.

But we were a talented team that was often underestimated.

We had some solid years and started to gain some traction. A strong core of younger guys was rising in the league—guys like myself, Tyler Bozak, Jake Gardiner, and Matt Frattin. We were the up-and-comers; all of us were in the American League together on a team that made a deep run for the Calder Cup. I had a special bond with those guys. Joffrey Lupul, too, was a great player at the time.

We also benefited from some great veteran leadership in guys like Phil and Dion. I respected the hell out of each of them. And, as I've already said, I was a big fan of Colton Orr—a big tough guy who always had my back. James Reimer was stepping it up in goal, earning his Optimus Reim reputation. That nickname has stuck with him to this day.

I grew close with Phil, one of purest goal scorers I've ever played with. He was a great teammate—passionate and dedicated but misunderstood and unfairly characterized by the media. The guy scored more than four hundred goals in his career and went on to win three Stanley Cups. It's baffling to me that he's never seemed to get the respect he deserves.

And Dion was one of the best captains I've ever played for. He was the kind of guy you want leading a room—a great leader who'd go out of his way for the boys. And as someone who demanded accountability from his teammates, he was also the kind of guy you never wanted to let down. Yet Dion took a lot of heat in Toronto. Obviously he had that "C" on his chest and the fans and media had to come down on somebody, but at times those criticisms were unwarranted.

The team had what was often referred to as a "good room," meaning we got along well and had a good time together. Sometimes, I'll admit, maybe too good. We were young guys who were professional but also liked to have fun.

We'd go to some sick parties in Toronto and got to enjoy a red-carpet lifestyle there for a few years. The bunch of us would go everywhere, to all the high-end nightclubs and some private parties, for instance at the Toronto International Film Festival. It'd be four a.m., last call, and we'd still be having a great time. We'd hang out with celebrities and go to movie premieres. It was cool just to have such a great group of guys to be able to share that with.

The attention I received in Toronto intensified every year I was there. I was lucky to be one of the fans' favourites, which I was so appreciative of. I've always loved Leafs Nation. There were some out there who didn't believe in me, of course. I wasn't super appreciative of that. But for the most part the fans seemed to respect the way I played.

You couldn't go anywhere or do anything without someone asking for a picture or autograph, which I was always happy to provide—as long as it was an appropriate time and place for it. In Toronto, most people were kind and respectful. They'd come up to chat, shake your hand, or ask for a photo.

Whenever we went out with the guys, we had to be careful, though. We'd always run into shit disturbers who'd go out of their way to act tough and give us a hard time. There'd be a few scumbags hopped up on liquid courage—they'd almost always be shitfaced, barely able to stand up—and giving us the gears. There they were, instructing us in how to play hockey, telling us why we suck, looking to get into some sort of fight, a story to tell their boys. It was hard to bite your tongue; sometimes you'd just want to go and smack the guy right in the mouth. But obviously you wouldn't be able to do that.

We were taught relatively early on that there'd be those who'd try to get under your skin. And that if you react the way you want to, there'd likely be a lawsuit—so be careful. All that kind of stuff. So whenever that did happen, we knew to just get out of there and keep moving.

And even apart from those approaching us outright, it was hard to maintain our privacy whenever we were out. We got caught a couple of times, and not because we were doing anything we shouldn't have. But if you're out and about at a questionable time or place, coaches could get a little sensitive about it. We chose our spots nicely and we weren't acting like idiots, but obviously if you're found at a bar or a nightclub and someone snaps a photo, the next thing you know they're telling the GM. And there are a lot of people in the industry who are, quite frankly, rats and snitches.

It would make you a little jaded. Some of those you thought you could trust, you clearly couldn't. As you get older you start to weed those people out, but when you're young, you're naive and think you can trust everybody.

Every once in a while you'd get called into a meeting. They'd say, "Hey, we know you were at this place, we know what time you got there, we know what time you left."

Busted.

I'd always be thinking, "How the fuck did you guys know?"

The hockey community is big and yet small at the same time. The informants get spotted quickly. It's just one of those things. As with any other job, there are guys who are like that, who take pride in giving out information.

AS THE FRUSTRATION MOUNTED on the ice, we tended to blow off a little more steam. And in the second half of the 2014–2015 season—the last year of my bridge deal—we fell into another tailspin. It was a difficult time.

Brendan Shanahan had taken over as president in spring 2024 and basically promised to put the team through a scorched earth rebuild. That January, Randy Carlyle was fired amid a stretch of losses. Assistant coach Peter Horachek took over as interim head coach.

The writing was on the wall. No one knew exactly what would happen, but we knew big changes were coming. It was disturbing, especially since we had such a great group. Yet when something that dramatic happens—when you don't win—change is inevitable.

MEANWHILE I WAS STILL VERY young and immature in my career, still trying to figure out how to navigate in the NHL, all eyes on you in Toronto. That's no excuse, of course. I should have known better.

In early March, the St. Louis Blues clobbered us 6–1 at home. We were completely in the dump. So after getting throttled I ended up going out late on King Street West with a few buddies, looking to shake it off. The night turned into a bit of a bender. I don't remember what time I went to bed, but I'll never forget when I woke up.

I didn't hear my alarm. Later, I rolled over and looked at the clock. Instant panic.

"Fuck."

Peter had called a team meeting for nine that morning.

I looked at my phone: about twenty missed calls. That's never a good sign.

Then I checked my texts. There were another dozen or so from teammates, all echoing the same sentiment: *Where the fuck are you?*

"Fuck. This is bad news," I thought. Especially after we'd been shit-kicked the night before.

I ran out the door with virtually one leg inside my pants, trying to get there as quickly as possible. I must have driven a hundred miles an hour, freaking out, to the practice rink in Etobicoke.

I parked and sprinted into the building, thinking there might still be a chance to make it in time. I opened the dressing room door. Everyone was there. The coaches stood by the whiteboard. It was mid-meeting. The entire room looked up at me. It was dead silent.

It felt like one of those nightmares where you show up to school for a presentation, look down, and realize you're naked. Except this was real. And this was much, much worse.

I inched toward a corner of the room with my head down, trying to be subtle. It didn't work. Before I got to my seat, Peter Horachek decided he'd had enough of my sad attempt to sneak in as though nothing had happened.

"Get. The. Fuck. Out!" he shouted. In case I didn't understand the message, he added, "Leave. Go Home."

"Oh no," I thought. I left the room and started to panic. My mind started spinning: "I fucked up. This is not good."

It was not even a little funny at that moment.

I hung around the rink for a bit, not sure what to do—as if Peter hadn't been clear enough. After awkwardly trying to keep myself busy, I gave up and went home to await my fate. My phone rang. It was Brendan Shanahan, hockey legend and president of the Leafs. My stomach sank. Shanny was calm on the phone. He just told me to come in for a meeting the next morning. My stomach remained on the floor.

I didn't sleep at all that night. But I set about a dozen alarms, just in case I did.

The next morning I felt as if I were walking into my own execution. I met Shanny in his office. It was a brief meeting, not really even a discussion. The team, he said, was suspending me for three games. There wasn't much else to say—it's not as though I had a defence. I walked away knowing I'd fucked up and that I'd have to win back whatever trust the team had had in me.

The locker room was tense that day. The guys were nice, but this was serious, and not something to joke about. (They would later, of course—for years I was given a hard time about sleeping in.)

As disappointed as I knew the coaching staff, the front office, and most importantly my teammates were in me, it couldn't compare to the disappointment I had in myself. I was crushed. How could I have done something so stupid? It was a small thing, maybe—but it felt enormous, especially given how our games had gone to that point. We were in the middle of an absolute tire fire of a season.

Dion Phaneuf ripped into me in the way a captain should. And Dion was someone I respected, so his words really resonated. In the end, he was one of the best people to talk to about it: he gave me a real wake-up call, and I learned a lot from him about accountability.

Then he defended me publicly. He told reporters I'd handled myself well through it all and that the team would support me. I so appreciated that, but was sorry to have put him in a position to have to answer those questions at all.

For a couple of days speculation about why I'd been suspended ran rampant. News leaked about the missed meeting, but the Leafs didn't fill in the blanks. They left it up to me to speak to the media about it, which I did. After all, I was accountable for my own actions. I had to face the questions, embarrassing as the experience was.

IN MY SECOND GAME BACK following that suspension, I ran into more trouble after a hit on Edmonton's Matt Fraser. It was an unintentional collision on a typical hockey play. When Fraser went behind our net to play the puck, I cut in from the opposite side. Then, right before I reached him, he turned as he backhanded the puck around the boards. I was going too fast to stop, so at the last second I tried to squeeze between them and Fraser. But as I pulled in, my shoulder connected with Fraser's head and he went down hard. It was an ugly scene. I immediately stopped and put my hand on his chest as the refs blew the play dead. The other Oilers came after me right away, which I got, and yet I was just trying to make sure Matt was all right. I was given a two-minute minor on the ice for the hit.

Then the NHL's Department of Player Safety called us up. I was back in hockey court—and this time they went overboard in their review. I was given four games, which, considering the specifics of the play, was bullshit.

The suspension was the culmination of a snowball effect, coming as it did after I'd been suspended for three games the season before.

That one was for elbowing Minnesota Wild goalie Niklas Bäckström in the back of the head, and it too was completely unintentional. It followed a routine play during which Joffrey Lupul took a shot on net from the top of the circle. I followed the puck from the right side of the goal and tipped the shot with my stick into Bäckström's pads. It was crowded in front. There were two Wild guys around me. I tried to jump by Bäckström, but I was in tight. I went through his crease, for sure. My intention was to dodge him, but in doing so I accidentally got my forearm raised and it hit him. Bäckström ended up missing some time, which was terrible. I felt bad about that. But it had just been the regular bang-bang type stuff you encounter in hockey. Sometimes you lose track of where you are on the ice. I really didn't mean to hit him.

During my hearing with the league, I admitted that I should have been more aware of the impending collision. The league said I'd been in complete control of the play and hadn't been steered into him, but that they also believed it wasn't intentional. I'd been watching the puck the entire time, turning to the goal only after I tipped the puck. And given my momentum, when I turned I was already on top of Bäckström. To limit contact I tucked in my elbow, but it was too late. Then, as I fell after the collision, my arm flared out—which many people viewed as my attempt to hit him but was just the force of the fall. The league agreed with that.

You never want to see someone get injured, but it happens. Still, the play was my responsibility, and I did the time for it. And in addition to the four-game suspension, I was put on an eighteen-month probation, meaning I'd get a tougher penalty if I did something like that again within that time. The hit on Fraser was seventeen months later.

I was sorry Matt had gotten hurt on the play, and that was my biggest concern. I hoped he was okay.

It was the lowest point of my career. I still felt terrible about the team-issued suspension the season before, and now I was not only back in the headlines but off the ice for another four games.

The season came to a merciful end a couple of weeks later. By that time we'd put up six wins and thirty losses since the beginning of January. It was a demoralizing, humiliating finish.

AND THAT FINISH WAS MADE worse by the fact that we knew this was pretty much the end for our group. Dave Nonis and Peter Horachek were fired after the regular season ended. Brendan Shanahan's rebuild would start in the off-season.

It had to happen, but it was still a tough pill to swallow. If you don't get the job done, you know changes are coming. That's difficult to think about because you want to see your buddies in a good situation. And these were some of my close pals, guys I'd seen every single day for nine months straight; we'd formed such good relationships that they'd become almost like family. Then one day, at the snap of a finger, they're signed somewhere else, or traded, or released, and you're not going to see them that often anymore.

Of course, some people you have a better bond with than others. It's easier to stay in touch. I'm still very good buddies with several of the guys from those Toronto days—Bozak, van Riemsdyk, Gardiner. Morgan Rielly, who was then a second-year guy. Dion. Phil. I've stayed in contact with them all. That's when you know you had a special group, when years down the road you're still chatting.

Other guys are more like co-workers. You work together as a team, trying to achieve the same goals, pulling on the same rope. But you go from seeing each other every single day, all day—on the road, at home, sitting in a hot tub. Then suddenly they're gone and you never talk to them again.

That happens in a lot of cases, probably more so than the ones where you keep in touch. It's an interesting dynamic—but that's the reality of pro sports.

AS SUMMER APPROACHED, it was clear that a new era was about to begin.

In May, after signing a massive eight-year, $50 million deal, Mike Babcock became the Leafs' head coach. That June, the team drafted Mitch Marner first overall. Then on July 1, the first day of free agency, Phil Kessel was traded to the Pittsburgh Penguins. And a few days later I signed a one-year extension worth $4.1 million, feeling very much that my future with the organization was uncertain.

16
PROVING IT

LOU LAMORIELLO AND MIKE BABCOCK sat on the couch in my parents' living room.

"What is going on here," I wondered. "Is this normal?"

It seemed like a bizarre dream. I was so nervous.

In the summer of 2015, Lamoriello—one of the most experienced executives in the game—was hired as the Leafs' general manager. Babcock had already inked the most lucrative coaching contract in NHL history.

And having just signed that one-year extension, my future with the Leafs depended entirely on the two men now devouring my mother's Lebanese snacks while my father chatted confidently about the state of the franchise.

They'd driven out to London to meet us, having told me they wanted to see me at home and get to know my world a little better— to know where I came from and what made my personality tick.

I think everyone in my family was nervous, except my father.

He was his typical confident self. Calm, cool, and collected. The business guy.

My mother, who is incredibly shy, was freaking out.

She'd fretted over what to offer them. Our culture is very hospitable when someone comes over, so she was in the kitchen firing up every delicious snack she could think of—and she kept them coming, too, snack after snack, hardly saying a word in the process.

I'd been with the Leafs for five seasons, but even then it was a bit of a surreal experience to have Lou and Babs there in my family home.

Over coffee and snacks we talked about the direction of the team and the direction of me. These two guys were coming in to change the franchise. I understood that, and I wanted to be a part of it. We ended up having a great discussion. It was all pretty casual; we even had the TV on. And Babs didn't ask me to put any of my photos on airplay for a family slideshow, which helped keep things comfortable.

I think they both realized then how much I wanted to be part of the franchise. It was clear that they were just there to do their homework.

Again: *I had Mike Babcock and Lou Lamoriello sitting on my couch.*

"Shit, this is weird," I thought for the umpteenth time.

It was a crossroads in my career. I tried to hold on to the mindset that I'd just go out there, do what I loved to do, and try not to think about it. But I'd be lying if I said the pressure didn't get to me. The team suspension at the end of the last season had put me on notice.

In my mind there were only two directions I could go: either push through the tribulations and come out on top or fade into being just another player. I was all for the former, of course. The controversies weighed heavily, but I tried not to let it affect me—and I'd always been pretty good at narrowing my focus and concentrating on what I needed to.

That summer I knew I'd have to solidify my position with the Leafs. I'd finished the season fourth in scoring with eighteen goals and twenty-one assists in seventy-three regular-season games. By that time I'd played exactly 250 NHL games, with 152 points. And now I'd just signed that one-year extension deal. So it would be a big year for me, since if I didn't perform I'd probably end up somewhere else.

It wasn't like nowadays, where the trend seems to be that kids come out of their entry-level deal and sign an eight-year contract. Back then it was different. Management's message was "Prove it, prove it, prove it." You constantly had to justify yourself. Year in, year out, and even if you'd had a monster campaign, the message was still "Do it again. We don't think you can."

I didn't have that much leverage, except to play well enough that the team had no choice but to keep me. I'd been in that position before.

Back then, the guys running these franchises didn't like to commit to long-term contracts. Especially for young players, who they felt had to show them everything they had before they could earn a long-term deal. There was constant doubt from the organization. And that never sat right with me, since it was clear that they didn't believe in me as much as I believed in myself.

So there I was, with a one-year contract, betting on myself again. But once you sign your deal, you have to honour it. And I was committed to bringing the Leafs my best.

In the end, when Babs and Lou left, I felt it had gone pretty well. I was happy to have shared my world with them, to have them experience what my family was all about. And I think they respected it, and that it made them feel better about who I actually was as opposed to the image that had been constructed for me. Lou had gotten to know my family, and he seemed to enjoy our dynamic. He understood that I had a great support system. I believe that's one of the reasons why he came to like me so much.

THAT 2015–2016 SEASON WAS EFFECTIVELY a tryout for the Leafs' new era. William Nylander had been drafted in 2014, eighth overall, and Marner had been taken fourth earlier in 2015. Neither would join the club for another season. But we'd signed the most sought-after head coach in recent history, and Lamoriello was busy finding the pieces he needed. Everything was set for an effective rebuild.

Meanwhile, Toronto was home for me, and I was ready to give the franchise everything I had. I wanted more than anything to be a part of what was being built.

The season went as expected. We broke the franchise record for most losses in a season, with fifty-three. Phaneuf was traded to Ottawa in February, along with Matt Frattin. James Reimer was traded to the San Jose Sharks amid a flurry of trades focused on positioning us to compete down the road.

I led the team in scoring and penalty minutes, with seventeen goals and twenty-eight assists for forty-five points—along with seventy minutes in the habbis.

I'D ENJOYED PLAYING FOR MIKE Babcock, who could be a controversial guy but who definitely knew his shit. We had a pretty good relationship, and I think he realized early on that I wasn't a player he could bully.

The first time I met him, he'd just signed his eight-year contract and I'd just signed my one-year deal. He brought me into the office one day to introduce ourselves and chat for a bit. One of the first things he said was something like "Listen, I just signed for eight years." It was a "we're going to do things my way or the highway" type of thing.

"Well, Babs," I said, "I'm not going anywhere either."

So, whereas others had a much more difficult time with him, I think our dynamic worked because we understood each other.

Of course, we certainly had our moments when we'd "motherfucker" each other. But we'd always hash it out the next day. He knew I had a fierceness that he couldn't really take advantage of and that I was going to tell him how it was and how I was feeling. And I think Babs respected that.

And in the end he made me a better player, both in my attention to detail and in the X's and O's of the game. He really helped round out my play. Plus, he was very well prepared. That's one thing I think anyone he's coached would say about him. He always had a game plan. His X's and O's were probably the best I've seen.

Babcock also knew how to motivate. One day he brought me into the office to say he had aspirations for me as a top two-way player. He believed I could be a Selke Trophy winner—which Pavel Datsyuk had won three years in a row in Detroit—and asked if I wanted to play like Datsyuk. He must have known how much I admired him.

"Of course," I said. "I want to be exactly like him."

I was a huge Datsyuk fan, and Babcock had coached him for years with the Red Wings. One of the assistant coaches who came with Babs from Detroit had even brought me one of his sticks. I loved to look at players' sticks to check out the curve, lie, and flex. I was a nerd about that kind of stuff. Datsyuk had a couple things on his stick I noticed, and I copied these. To this day, my stick has those same details.

That's just an example of how Babcock was into that psychology thing. He knew what he was doing from a mental standpoint. Sometimes he'd go offside, but a lot of the time there was a method to his madness. He gave me some advice on how to play more like Datsyuk did, advice I really appreciated. Babs was calculated like that; he loved those motivational tactics and would always try to give players a spark to get the best out of them.

I'd pretended to be Datsyuk for years through minor hockey. Now, all of a sudden, I was inspired to play like Datsyuk again. It was a way for Babcock to press the right buttons and get me going—along with his mention of the Selke Trophy and the two-way centre. I was all in.

Having told Babs I wanted those things, I was determined to be true to my word, so I had to elevate my game. And that ended up being my true coming out party, as I was able to demonstrate that I could play with anyone.

Babcock put me out against the opponent's top line every night. I had a pretty good year. I'd go toe to toe with some of the best players in the league, determined not to get embarrassed. That keeps you firing. You want to be the kind of player your coaches can count on. You want to be known as someone who can get the job done. And the fact that they trust you with that kind of assignment makes you believe in yourself. I'd always been a kid with a ton of pride. So sending me out against the top line was a way to get me engaged every single night, to understand that if I wasn't on I'd get embarrassed. And I wasn't going to let that happen.

But Babcock also gave me my share of shit. That first year he coached me, during the 2015–2016 season, I was in the guy's office every day. He would not leave me alone. Every day he'd be telling me something about how I could improve my game. It was all about the details. It got to a point where I was thinking, "Holy fuck—I don't want to be in your office every single day." But that's how Babs was: very hands on. And I think he understood the type of person who could rise to the challenge. He pushed me, and it worked.

You could even say he made me a bit of a project, with the result that I became a better two-way player. In fact it was during that season that I developed into a complete, well-rounded player for the first time. I knew I'd always had that offensive ability, that flair and flash. But this was when I really started to focus on what it took to win games. I began thinking about the finer points involved in how to win faceoffs and in how to build a defensive game that'll make you hard to play against.

I became a very detailed player after that. It wasn't all because of Babs. I'd always been aware of my weaknesses and worked hard each year to address them. I was driven to improve. I had a lot of pride and wanted to be a guy my teammates could trust. That attention to detail is what being a professional is all about. It's what helps make you a key piece on a team in pursuit of a championship.

There were also a lot of things Babcock did that I didn't agree with. He'd try to hold everybody else accountable for their actions, and sometimes he had to be held accountable for his own.

That's how great teams operate.

THROUGH THE SECOND HALF OF our season, as the fire sale continued and as we limped toward our lowly end, Lou Lamoriello was at the stage where he knew all the players and had evaluated our play. He had a vision for the team, which we all knew meant that things were going to change. We had one of the worst records in the league. It was time to flip the script. That was inevitable.

Players and personnel alike were walking on eggshells, all of us unsure about what might happen.

The last night of the year, after the regular season was over, we all went out for our team party in Toronto. During it I got a call from Lou saying he wanted to meet with me the following morning at eight—which was pretty early after a team party.

"Shit," I thought. "What does this guy want to talk about?"

I had no contract. I was a restricted free agent and had no idea what was going to happen the next season. So my mind was in a pretzel, trying to figure out what Lou wanted to discuss. After that call I can't say I enjoyed the team party as much as I would have otherwise. I was freaking out all night.

The next morning, it was just Lou and I in his office. Knowing I was one of the players who enjoyed the city's nightlife, he asked who else I'd gone out with. And who exactly was doing what and where?

My back was against the wall. I was coming off a pretty decent year, but it hadn't been spectacular. My whole body was stiff, tight with anxiety. Lou had me by the balls. He wanted names, he wanted places. A full interrogation. I was sweating.

I knew a bunch of names. I knew what everyone was up to. We all did.

"I don't know anything about it," I lied. "I have no idea what you're talking about. I only know about me."

Lou looked at me as if I were the worst liar on the planet. He saw right through me. But I wasn't about to throw anyone under the bus to save my own ass. I didn't even know if my ass was savable at that point anyway.

"It's not good for you," he warned me.

I left the room terrified.

"I'm fucked," I thought.

I pictured Lou sitting in his chair saying, "See you later, Naz. You're playing for a different team next year."

He was testing me. I'm convinced he already knew all the information he was asking me to give him. Lou was legendary for his CIA-level intel. He was always keeping an eye on the boys. There was nothing you did that he didn't know about.

But I hadn't named a soul. I didn't crack. I stood by my teammates.

By my own standards, I'd passed with flying colours.

But at the same time, I sure as hell got the message. When the Godfather tells you something *isn't good for you*, you listen.

For the next few days, I thought I was gone. I was almost certain my time in Toronto was done. Lou left me hanging.

17
A NEW ERA BEGINS

IN RETROSPECT, I THINK THAT was the turning point for me and Lou.

He didn't know me at all when he came in. But he didn't seem to let preconceived notions about my character shade his perception of me. Lou gave people a chance to prove themselves. He made his own judgments.

He seemed to respect the way I'd carried myself in that meeting, knowing full well he had me cornered. And when you have someone in a position like mine, with an uncertain future and everything to lose, you know you're going to see his true character.

A couple of weeks later, in mid-April, I signed a six-year deal worth $27.5 million. As I signed my name I thought of all the times I'd been told I'd be nothing more than a minor leaguer. None of those guys had remained in the organization. It was vindication.

I was happily locked into Toronto now. I'd gone from being as scared about my future with the club as I'd ever been to seeing myself possibly spending my entire career as a Leaf. And at the time, that was all I wanted.

THAT SPRING WE ENDED UP with a top-five pick in the NHL draft and won the first overall pick in the lottery. With Marner and Nylander ready to start their rookie years with us, it finally felt like there was excitement around the club again. This would be a new era for the Leafs, a culture change—that's how the team sold it. We were set to become winners.

There was a debate at that time about who the Leafs would take first overall, Patrik Laine or Auston Matthews. Laine, a stud before he even got to the NHL, was a serious consideration. So back then the conversation was a lot tighter than most people remember.

Babcock called me before the draft to say they were planning to take Matthews but wanted to know what I thought.

"Yes," I said. "It's a no-brainer."

I was completely on board with taking Matthews and I was honoured that Babs asked me what I thought. I felt good about that kind of communication. It was going to be me and Matthews as the one-two punch up the middle, so it meant a lot to be asked about a decision that would impact our future, even if, in hindsight, it was an obvious one. It seemed my opinion mattered to the organization, which was a huge shift from my early years with the franchise.

Matthews had a confidence about him, which I loved, because I had a similar swagger. I loved his belief in himself. It was clear that he was special from the moment I stepped on the ice with him, before he even played a professional game. And then obviously he goes out in his first game and scores four goals and puts up 40 in his rookie season.

Everyone knows Matthews is a goal scorer. He's a big guy who can skate well, with a tremendous amount of skill. But I think what sets him apart are the little details in his game, like most of hockey's greatest players. He knows where to be. He can anticipate plays and almost be a step ahead of them. He's good around the net and can find different ways to score. It's not always a one-timer, bar down. He scores on wraparounds and rebounds. He's just so effective and lethal.

He also handled the pressure of being a first overall pick in Toronto tremendously well. He never let the bright lights bother him. He'd obviously been highly touted as a player since he was young, so he was somewhat prepared for it. As much as a young player can be, anyway. From the start he made it clear that he could step up when he needed to. And on the rare occasion that he didn't, he was able to shrug it off and not really worry about what other people were saying.

Mitch was like the Energizer Bunny. He's funny, he's entertaining—he's got an unbelievable personality. Anyone who gets to know him knows that he is an easy guy to like. He was always one of my favourite teammates to be around. He's the complete package; he brings the energy, he brings the skill, he brings the humour, and he brings a party.

Mitch gets a lot of shit in the Toronto market, which comes with being a high-money guy on the Leafs, but I don't think the vitriol he's faced is justified. He's a remarkable talent and he's a competitive little prick. He works his ass off and hates to lose. He does everything properly.

As a player, I'd take him on my team all day, every single day on any team I play for. If I'm building a team, he's the guy that I want on my team.

Back then, when that new Leafs era really began, there was a lot to be excited about. Big things were coming. Auston Matthews was eighteen, Mitch Marner was nineteen, and Willie Nylander was twenty. Suddenly, at twenty-five, I was one of the older guys in the group. We had a good mix of young talent and veteran players. And with several guys who had more veteran status than I did, I fit into a key role in the club, still reaching my prime. There's a point, usually after your entry-level contract and when you've got a couple hundred games under your belt, when you feel like an established presence in the league. Having reached that point, I felt confident about where I was.

We meshed well as a team that season. The young guys fit in right away. It was clear that they were team guys.

One notable test of that commitment was passed at the annual rookie party. The gatherings always followed a common script. The rookies always pay for dinner and they have to stand up and tell some jokes. That's tradition.

When I was a rookie, I had to wear a full-body banana costume all night—through dinner, and as we all went out to the bar afterwards. I tried to take it off multiple times but was unsuccessful. I remember being in a packed nightclub, feeling ridiculous in this sweaty yellow banana costume.

In 2016, one of our rookies rocked the best flow the league had seen since the days of Guy Lafleur. William Nylander loved his hair, for good reason. The lettuce on this kid was like Goldilocks. It was an easy target for us. We surprised him after the rookie dinner, telling him we were going to shave his head. We sat him down in a chair, put a barber cape around his neck and pulled out a pair of clippers. You could see his heart drop to his stomach. He was absolutely devastated, but he was a good sport about it. He didn't put up a fight. Not that he had much of a choice. We plugged in the clippers and turned them on. We were committed to the act, but we didn't go through with it. We weren't monsters. Who could destroy a head of hair like that?

THAT 2016–2017 SEASON ALSO MARKED the first time when I truly felt I played a valued role as a leader of the club. And it was Lou Lamoriello who instilled that confidence in me.

A lot of people are intimidated by him. There's this sort of myth about Lou being a hardass. But he and I got along very well, especially after that interrogation in his office and after I'd signed my big contract with the club. And over the following months, I think we kind of bonded in a way.

Eventually guys on the team would start giving me a hard time about that, calling me "Lou's son." We seemed to get each other, which I think most fans might find interesting, considering how he's often viewed as the Godfather of the Old School.

Lou understood me, he respected me, and he liked the way I played the game. He was very fond of me. At that time I was going through a period of growing maturity in my life, and he didn't hold that sometimes-faltering process against me. He saw what kind of player and what kind of man I could become—and that trust meant everything to me.

He had that old Italian man mentality. Lou was classy, but also stubborn and very direct. I loved him. He's still one of the greatest people I know. He'd always go out of his way to come over and chat with me, ask how I was doing, how my family was. He knew how much they meant to me, and I think he approved of that. He knew firsthand how great my parents were and that I'd been raised right.

But it took some time to build that relationship. He tried to get a sense of what I was made of early on. Once he realized that I was a quality person and a good player, he really stood up for me and had my back. It was nice to have someone like that in your corner.

Lou was skilled at assessing character and who to surround yourself with. That's one of the many things I give him credit for. He did his due diligence, finding out who would benefit the group and who wouldn't. As players, once your team is set, you rally with each other and just try to make that situation work as well as it possibly can. We had no trouble doing that with this squad. It was a good room.

We saw Lou every single day. Not only was he very much involved in the day-to-day operations of the club, but he also joined us on every flight and attended pretty much every one of our road games. He was around a lot. I think that's what made him so acute in reading the dynamics and in understanding what's good for the dressing room and what's not. He saw everything.

Lou also put players through a lot of mental tests. When coaches or management are trying to understand what players to acquire, keep, or trade, they put them in difficult situations to see how they react. It's a kind of mental warfare, these psychological games. But that's how professional sports are—you're trying to get down to the bottom of something positive, to find out someone's true character when their back is against the wall and they have nowhere to go. That's when you find out who someone really is. And Lou just had a way to sniff that out. It's no surprise that he's been around championship players and on championship teams.

MIKE BABCOCK, TOO, WAS NOTORIOUS for the mind games he'd play. But he and Lou were two different types of personalities. Lou liked to assess people's character, but Babcock liked to push buttons in order to see what would make people crack. I think he did it to get the most out of his players, but it often backfired.

As I've said, Babs and I also had a pretty good relationship; he knew I wasn't going to take shit from him. But he would go after guys who were in vulnerable positions, and sometimes he took it too far.

The Mitch Marner story is the most well-known example of how that could blow up in Babcock's face.

Mitch was just a kid that season, still trying to fit in with the group as a rookie and get his teammates to like him. Mitch is a great guy. We were both Knights alumni and got along very well. There's nothing unlikable about him. But right from the start he faced a lot of pressure as a high draft pick, part of the promise of this new era for the team. Given that pressure, I always thought he carried himself nicely, especially as a hometown kid. It's amazing how much shit a guy can take just for being an incredibly talented player. So I wanted to make sure he felt welcomed into the team, and to guide him in the way guys like Phil Kessel and Dion Phaneuf had done for me.

The Babcock incident happened on a road trip in New Jersey. It was what we called a "Dad's trip," meaning our fathers were tagging along, which was special for us all. I'm sure it was an exciting time for Mitch, having his dad join us.

But Babs ruined that. He stepped out of line big time when he asked Mitch to make a list of the most and the least hardworking guys on the team. And he didn't mean just a few names at the top and bottom; he wanted a list from one to twenty-three, all the guys on our roster. Of course, in doing something like that, you're going to have to throw some people under the bus. Mitchy was not that kind of kid. This was the last thing he'd ever do, and he wanted no part of it. Regardless, Babcock made him do it.

And afterward, he showed the rankings to some players. I'm not sure if it was a large group of guys or just a few individually, but either way, guys caught wind of the list. Mitch felt terrible about it. He ended up telling us the story—almost confessing in a way. I could tell that it was eating away at him.

What a bullshit position to put a player in, let alone a rookie. It's not as though Babs was asking a veteran who could push back and say "Fuck you, I'm not doing that." Mitch obliged, feeling pressured—forced, really—to do what Babs wanted. When Mike Babcock is your coach and it's your rookie season, if he tells you to do something you're probably going to do it.

When we found out, Tyler Bozak and I stormed into Babcock's office and laid into him. He tried to defend what he'd done, to explain the thought process behind the exercise. But there wasn't much he could say, and in the end I think he realized he'd made a mistake. After that he apologized to Mitch. We'd pretty much made him.

We had Mitchy's back. He'd been put in a tough spot, and you just don't do that to a rookie. He wasn't himself for the next couple of days. Everyone knew what had happened and the kind of shit Babcock would pull, so we tried to make him feel better about it.

I talked earlier about the old-school way of coaching and how much it's changed. And here was a classic situation where the old-school approach was clashing with the new reality.

Even though Babs apologized, the damage was done. But after that he was more strategic in the way he did things. He certainly crossed swords with other players, but he seemed a little more careful about it—he knew now that there could be pushback.

Still, it wasn't the last time Babcock would share information we considered private. Another incident that rubbed some of the guys the wrong way happened when Babcock called a meeting with the team and the entire training staff in the same room. He'd asked all the trainers to rank players on the level of effort they put into their gym routines—green being good, yellow being average, and red being mediocre.

There was an assumption that the information would be kept confidential, but Babcock brought up each assessment, one by one, in front of the entire team. The whole point was to embarrass guys, and it made for some awkward conversations between the players and the training staff. Once you break that trust it's hard to come back, so it was all a bit of a shitshow.

It was a tense time, for sure. But in the end everyone hashed it out, since we all knew that moving forward was what was best for the team.

Babs was really into the psychological aspects of performance. He'd been a psychology major at McGill University, a fact that everyone seemed to know. As I've said, he was interested in ways to motivate players, to get the most out of them by knowing what buttons to press, what games to play. All that kind of stuff.

But over a long period of time, that can wear on you, and so these kinds of coaches often have a shelf life. Obviously, there was some benefit because Babs had a lot of success. He was a brilliant coach. But again, his tactics could also backfire. And with players having changed so much over the past decade, there's no longer a place in the league for mind games like that.

18

SKILLS THERE ARE
NO TROPHIES FOR

YEAR BY YEAR, AS YOUR career unfolds, you start to think about how you're going to stay on top of your game as you age. A lot of it is having a good mentality. Every player in the league is in great shape and everyone has an incredible skill set, so what can really set you apart is how you think about the game: how you can bounce back from a mistake, how you can get past a shitty game and not let it snowball. Being able to avoid that is part of what separates the good players from the great.

The best players make mistakes, just as everyone does. But they have the courage to not worry about making that mistake again—and the mental toughness to go out the next time and try the exact same thing but execute it a little better, make it happen that time.

I've carried a simple saying with me throughout my career: "When the going gets tough, you get tougher." If you have that mentality and that commitment, and if you stay with it consistently, taking care of your mindset, then eventually whatever setbacks you experience are going to be temporary.

Meanwhile, another sort of change happens as your career progresses. When you're first starting out, you're virtually a sponge. You try to be observant, to pick up on an admired player's personality, how they interact with teammates, how they execute a play on the ice. You're always looking for such examples to mimic, to help make you a better player and a better person. But then, as you evolve, you find ways to contribute to your team that don't always show up as glamorous stats. After all, there's much more to the game than goals and assists.

I'VE OFTEN BEEN NEAR THE top of the league in penalties drawn. My game has always had a quickness and a kind of elusiveness that forces guys to clutch and grab. So it's a compliment when I see myself up there in that stat, and even now I'm often near the top.

It's definitely a craft and a skill—and an underrated but important part of the game. Power plays, for example, are huge; I'm always looking to get that advantage. It's constantly having that unpredictable quality so that your opponents don't know what you're going to do. I think that's always been something I'm good at. It's about the illusion—the sneakiness.

But at the same time, it's also about getting gritty and getting under a player's skin, drawing him into a roughing penalty. In other words, just trying to be a prick out there, irritating guys whenever you can. I've been pretty good at that too over the years, so a few penalties have been drawn there as well. There's an art to it. Like a good comedian, you've got to have your material ready to go. And that means the players you play against: you make sure you know them well, and you keep tabs on what everyone's doing. It's all part of the preparation.

For my part, I don't really let words get to me. It's the old sticks-and-stones-may-break-my-bones adage. I'm much more likely to snap at players' actions. I don't get fazed too much by what they say; it's more about what they do.

I think the most dangerous opponents are the ones who talk shit—you know, the ones who are a bit tough, a bit gritty—but who can also make you pay on the scoreboard. That kind of player can irritate you the most: the guy who's chirping at you, and then all of a sudden he scores and you've got nothing to say. So I always try to bring in that dual element, just to wear on people.

Every player is different. For some, when they start getting into verbal arguments, it shows that they're frustrated, that they're getting off their game. For me it's always been the opposite. Having a verbal or physical altercation is a way to get myself into the game, to be engaged in the moment. I always become a little more focused when someone chirps because then you want to shove it right up their ass. That's always been the mentality for me. I want to score, I want to do something now, so I'll just unload on this guy. It's more of a pride thing.

Sometimes, of course, it doesn't work out in my favour. Those incidents are always a little embarrassing. But most of the time I'll take my chances. I've come out on the right side of that a lot, too. It's a bit of a gamble.

There's no trophy for penalties drawn. It's one of the details that don't go into the goals or points category but still has an impact on the game.

THE WAY I PLAY, I used to get chirped all the time. It didn't really affect me much. I usually found it funny more than anything. I've always loved that kind of confrontation—that verbal exchange between two guys who are fired up. I wished all the players were mic'd up. That would be an entertaining show. It's a fun dynamic to the game in professional sports. You're not going to hear anything like that working a desk job, so it's very unique.

I'll put myself up there with some of the best at getting guys off their game. I've had some pretty witty one-liners that people have heard over the years. That's the art of chirping. You have to be witty, you have to be on your toes. You have to have some material ready to go. That's always important.

One of the things they would constantly get me on was my suspensions. I'd always get chirped about that. People would go pretty low with that. It was a little touchy at times, especially when I was fresh off a suspension. But the more you hear it, the numbness just starts to set in and it doesn't really faze you anymore. I also learned to use it to my advantage. If I want to scare somebody a little bit, I'll remind them that I've been suspended before and I'm not afraid to be suspended again. I have a well-earned track record. You can see them thinking: "Yeah. He might do something stupid."

You try to flip it on them a little bit. That's always been something I've been good at. It's fun for me more than it is a sore spot.

Usually it's the enforcers who have the best chirps. They're the guys who can back it up, so it probably gives them a little more confidence in that department. You can't chirp if you're not confident, which is why chirping is an important part of the game. When you're intimidated, the chirping part of your brain shuts off. If you're in a rage, the chirping part of your brain shuts off. Anyone who can stand in there and chirp is *proving* they're not afraid and that their emotions are under control. No surprise then that the heavyweights are so good at it. Fearlessness and keeping their emotions under control is pretty much their day job. They are also usually among the smartest guys on the team. But there are always some skilled guys who are pretty sharp with the chirps as well.

When I was younger I was much less vocal on the ice than I became later on in my career. When you're still trying to make it in the league, you don't really have much to say. As a first-round pick in Toronto, there was a lot of attention around me—which of course puts a target on your back and gives the guys ammunition. I didn't get off to a great start in my career, which was well documented by the media. During a game against the Montreal Canadiens, I lined up on the wing across from Maxim Lapierre for the opening faceoff at the Bell Centre. Before the puck dropped, he leaned over to me.

"I thought you were going to be way better," he said. "You're not very good."

The best chirps are simple and right to the point. For a moment, I didn't know what to say. "Fuck," I thought. "That kind of sucks."

But I quickly regrouped. I wasn't about to just back down.

"Well, I always thought you were shitty." I said. "And you are pretty shit."

Maxim got the better of me there though. When he came after me, I got offended. "Fuck this guy," I thought. But it also stung a bit, as all good chirps do. It stayed with me—so much so, that it's still the first chirp that comes to mind whenever I think about the ones that stung the most over the years. Well played, Lapierre.

That kind of stuff happened on a pretty regular basis throughout my career.

I was too young to really be saying a whole lot. But when someone pissed me off, that's when I'd start to get yappy.

But there have also been times when I'd get a little too consumed by another player and throw myself off. That kind of frustration can creep up on you. And then suddenly you're a little too fired up.

Hockey is a fast, physical game. So you need to strike a balance between playing aggressively and potentially hurting someone. You never want that. And finding that equilibrium is something you learn with age and experience. It comes with maturity. I think there's a line: you don't want to overly frustrate yourself; you want to stay dialed in. You want to play as best you can, of course, and if you aren't able to achieve that balance, unhinged aggression will bite you in the ass.

I know that as well as anybody in the game today.

A slight miscalculation, or a movement you didn't anticipate, can lead to ugly plays. The margin of error is slim, but it's up to each player to make sure they don't make those mistakes.

Sometimes it looks a lot worse than it really is. But you've got to give a full account of what happened, to tell it like it is—whether there was contact to the head, for instance, or whatever the case may be. And I can honestly say that it has never, ever been my intention to hurt anyone. And none of the suspensions I've been given happened that way. I'm not saying it wasn't my fault or that the play wasn't dangerous or reckless. It absolutely was. Maybe I was a little angry at how they treated my teammate and I kind of just wanted to send a message but didn't do it in the proper fashion. That's something I've had to live with and be accountable for. But in each case it was the result of my failing to properly execute what I'd wanted to do. And that's something I've paid for.

Over the years I became a regular with the NHL's Department of Player Safety. It was always deserved, although I do feel that sometimes the punishment didn't really fit the crime.

There's a standard process. A hearing is held every time, and it's usually the general manager who tells you when it will take place. It's almost always done remotely, via a video call. They go over the tape, and you explain to the disciplinary person what happened. You're basically pleading your case. It's a lot like going to court, honestly. Then you wait a few hours while they reach a decision. You're completely at their mercy at that point.

That's the official sequence of events. Then there are the unwritten rules of the game.

Every time I stepped out of line and got suspended, I'd have someone coming after me in the game that followed, which is completely understandable. That game would always be circled on the team calendar. We all knew how it was going to play out. There'd be someone giving me shit for sure; there's always somebody to answer to. And that's a job for a certain kind of guy—to protect and enforce. These guys are bit out of my league in toughness, in what they bring as opposed to what I bring. But I've always been ready to answer the bell. Every single time there's been some sort of controversy, I take the heat in front of the cameras. I go back into their building and back on the ice, and if someone comes after me, I'm up for it. I understand. The other team is angry. They think what I did was bullshit, viewing it as being more intentional than it actually was. Regardless, they've taken issue with me—and I'm not going to back away from that.

That's what hockey is. That's what makes the sport so great.

As I've said, there's a grittiness to the way I play the game. And I'd much rather perform offensively than have to fight people. I think you have to put your foot down and stand up for yourself so that players will know they can't walk all over you. And that's what I did very early in my career. As valuable as my early lessons from players like Kessel and Phaneuf were, the education that Colton Orr gave me has always served me well.

When you're young in the league, you have to show that, especially if you're a skilled player, because guys will try to push you around. You have to fend for yourself. And eventually people will see that you're not going to be pushed around.

I've had to defend myself quite a few times over the years. I'd fight, I'd scrap, I'd do whatever I had to do to protect myself. If you want to sort it out, we'll sort it out. That's how it's always been. I don't care what you think about me, but that's something you've got to respect. I've never done something and then gone to hide in the corner afterward.

I DON'T GET INTO MANY fights, but I've had a few memorable tilts over the years.

I fought David Backes several times. We're both competitors, and we just seemed to clash whenever we faced off. Backes was an old-school, veteran guy. I was relatively young, trying to find my way. And I played with some grit. It might have rubbed some people the wrong way, which was intentional. Backes and I would go back and forth all the time.

It's funny because I have a lot of respect for him, although that doesn't really factor into what happens when someone has tossed off their gloves and is coming after you. Backes is a big man; I gave up about four inches and forty pounds to him.

Our first fight was epic. When he was captain of the St. Louis Blues, he called me out in front of everybody and maybe thought that he could push me around and embarrass me. But I ended up going toe to toe with him, on the road in St. Louis, in a hostile atmosphere. These are moments where opposing players will notice that even though a player can be a little rat out there, he's willing to answer the bell and stand up for himself. If you really don't want to have a guy like Backes making your life miserable every night, the only thing to do is to give it right back. It's no fun trying to intimidate a guy who doesn't skate away. The guy who stands in there wins just by not backing down.

I fought Backes again during his first game with the Boston Bruins. In that case he seemed to want to make a statement. I was happy to oblige. He had a job to do for his new team, and that job required punching me in the face. But I held my own against him, landing a good shot while taking a few. Over the years I probably fought him three times, and in their building, too. We always had a pretty even scrap.

For me, probably the most memorable fight was the Jumbo tilt of January 2018. We played the San Jose Sharks at home, which meant that Patrick Marleau, who'd joined us in the off-season, would be meeting up again with Jumbo Joe Thornton. The two had carved out iconic careers with the Sharks and were nearing their last days in the league.

Off the opening faceoff, I lined up against Jumbo, with Marleau on my wing. It was supposed to be a nice reunion. But we also had a game to win. And I had a chance to get inside the head of one of the game's all-time greats—a guy whose poster had been on my wall growing up. Of course I was going to take it.

We started jawing at each other as we lined up. There was a sequence of events leading up to this. I didn't really know Joe too well at the time. We battled for years. Every single time we played against each other, we were yelling at each other and whacking each other.

We both slashed each other's sticks anticipating the puck drop. As the ref reset we backed off, and after that we did it again—this time a little harder. Then Joe quickly whacked me in the arm, as if to say back off. In return I jabbed at his shin pads.

As the two of us got kicked out of the circle, we shared a few choice words. He asked me if I wanted to go.

"Fuck, Jumbo," I said. "I just got out of bed. Let me get into the game first."

"No, fuck you," he said. "Let's go."

At that point it was a given. No way was I going to back down, especially in our own rink at the start of the game. That was always my mentality. I've never been a guy to back down from anybody. Jumbo is a big boy, so it took me some courage. But at the end of the day, people respect it when you refuse to back down.

"Alright," I said. "Fuck it."

So as soon as the puck dropped we tossed away our sticks and went for it. Jumbo is a big man, four inches taller than me and about thirty pounds heavier. Plus his arms have to be twice as long as mine; I couldn't even reach across his shoulder.

Jumbo got a couple punches in as he grabbed on and then rag-dolled me as I fell off balance. I swung at him as I went down. The linesman was on top of us right away. Somewhere in the mix I got a piece of Joe's massive beard. I have no idea how, but I ended up with it in my hand. He didn't condition that mane well enough—it was dry and brittle. And when we got up there was a tumbleweed of grey hair lying on the ice.

It was a pretty funny scene in the end. And it not only fired up my teammates, it also got the Sharks' best player tossed in the box for the first five minutes of the game.

"I thought I was a hockey player, not a barber," I joked afterward.

Some people seemed to think I'd been disrespectful to Jumbo for getting into it with such an esteemed thirty-eight-year-old vet off the draw. The guy was a legend, but he was still a hockey player—and this was a hockey game. Jumbo himself didn't take issue with the scrap. But later my old coach Pete DeBoer—who was now running the Sharks—did.

"I love Naz," he said when he was asked about it. "I think with Joe Thornton, all I would say is I hope when Naz is thirty-eight and playing on reconstructed knees and had the career that Joe's had, that the next generation of players gives Naz the amount of respect that he deserves and has earned . . . That's a lesson."

Pete, who I love, was still trying to coach me, even when he was behind another team's bench! Anyway, he definitely knew me and did his best to play to what he saw as my weaknesses. He always tried to single me out. He'd send someone after me to try to get me off my game. I'd never shy away or back down. I'd always just want to shove it right up their ass. They basically tried to bully me, but I have way too much pride for that. I don't know if Pete really thought I shouldn't have fought Jumbo, but if the guy is asking me to fight in front of 20,000 people, I'm not going to get embarrassed.

And, Pete. When I'm thirty-eight, I promise I'll still be answering whatever challenge I'm given.

OUR SEASON ENDED IN DISAPPOINTMENT after we lost to the Boston Bruins in seven games in the first round—a result that would be viewed as constant as turning forward the clocks each spring.

But off the ice, it was an exciting time. My fiancé Ashley and I were married that July at Casa Loma in Toronto, an enormous castle-like estate with a stunning view of the city. We had the whole place to ourselves. The ceremony and speeches were inside the venue's massive historic library. Then we moved outside, where we set up a massive tent with a dance floor under the lights, with the Toronto skyline in front of us.

It was a perfect night—cool enough that we weren't just sweating through our shirts—and a perfectly clear sky.

And it was an all-timer of a party. Of course, my Lebanese heritage played a big part in the festivities. Middle Eastern weddings go hard, but my teammates were up to the challenge.

One of the traditions that is popular at Middle Eastern weddings is a dance called the Dabke. It involves holding hands in a line and dancing. It takes a lot of skill and experience to master the dance, but it's also fun for rookies to try. At a wedding you can learn a simple four-step dance while holding hands and moving in a circle.

My teammates had never done the Dabke before, so this was my chance to give them a little culture. They were feeling pretty loose, a few or seven cocktails in, and the beats were going. They joined in the Dabke like absolute beauties. It took them a few clumsy minutes to figure it out, but they're athletic boys.

I'll never forget seeing Auston Matthews, Mitch Marner, and William Nylander holding hands, following choreographed steps in a circle, giving it their absolute all. It meant a lot to me to see them embracing the moment and enjoying such a fun part of my culture. They were high-stepping by the end of it.

It was an absolute blast.

Through the course of an NHL career, weddings are often a chance to catch up with old teammates you haven't connected with in some time, but who still mean a lot to you even though they are now on the opposing side of the ice. Sometimes you even meet up with guys you battled with for years, and finally get a chance to have beer with.

Those guys all meant a lot to me. They'd been my teammates for several years and that group of guys had become close. A wedding is a celebration of family. And I know that family is a cliché that gets overused when we talk about our teammates, but this group really felt that close.

I'd battled alongside guys like Tyler Bozak, Leo Komarov, Morgan Rielly, and James Van Riemsdyk for years. Before my wedding JVR, Bozak and Komarov had all signed as free agents elsewhere. It was a bittersweet way to cap our time as Leafs together.

Fans rarely get to see beyond the serious, professional side of most teams. There is no way that they can really tell how well we get along from what they see on television or reported through the sports media. You're not going to understand the dynamics of a team from what reporters see when they are in a locker room, when it basically becomes a press-conference and everyone pretends it's not weird that we're walking around, getting dressed, or undressed. Because there is so much interest in a team like the Leafs, there is always a ton of speculation swirling around about who gets along with who in the locker room, and who doesn't. And it's almost always complete bullshit.

I saw those guys come up when they were rookies. It was cool to see them develop into the star players that they've become. And they're all such great guys on top of it.

Of course, I wasn't best friends with all my teammates, but in Toronto I certainly got along with all of them. This group meant so much to me. Some of that was because this was the only NHL team I'd ever known. At that point in my career, I fully wanted to be a Leaf until I retired. I couldn't imagine playing anywhere else. I loved my teammates, the team staff, the incredible fans, and the city. Toronto was home. But whenever teammates left for new opportunities, it was always a stark reminder that this is a business. You can battle along-side a guy for years, and the next season he's cross-checking you in the ribs when the ref isn't looking. But that doesn't change the fact that the bonds you form with teammates, even over a single season, are unique and meaningful.

Seeing these guys stumble through the Dabke at our wedding like absolute beauties was one of those moments in my career, in my life, that I'll never forget. That night was one of the best parties I've ever been to.

I ACTUALLY MET JUMBO FOR the first time at Mitch Marner's wedding, several years after our fight.

I introduced myself and met his wife. Everything was cool. It was like we were old friends. We had a good laugh about it.

"Remember that time I ripped a chunk of your beard out?"

"Oh yeah, that was hilarious."

That's the great thing about hockey. All of this animosity builds up on the ice and then you see them off the ice and it's like "Hey, what's up man? Everything good?" It's just that mutual respect. Everyone is competitive. Sometimes it gets a bit chippy. You understand that. Everybody who has been around knows that things happen and not to take anything too seriously.

And the thing is, our meeting at Mitch's wedding would have been far more awkward if I *had* avoided that scrap. Even if you are pissed off with a guy, squaring off is usually a sign of respect. It shows that no matter what got your tempers up, you have a lot in common, and that is the important thing. You don't lose respect for the guy who stands up for himself. It's the guy who slinks away that you might find it weird to hang out with at a friend's wedding.

19
BAD DECISIONS
FOR GOOD REASONS

I SAT AT THE BIGGEST boardroom table I'd ever seen in my life, sweating through my suit. More than two dozen people were in the room, all watching a giant screen showing the same replay in slow motion, frame by frame, on repeat.

How I'd come to be at NHL headquarters in New York City instead of getting ready for Game 3 of our first-round series against the Boston Bruins in the spring of 2019 is a bit of a complicated story.

Okay, not entirely that complicated. The reason I was at headquarters was right there on the screen, playing on repeat for representatives from the NHL, the NHLPA, and the Leafs, along with what seemed to be an extra dozen lawyer-type people tossed in for good measure. We were there because of the hit that looked worse and worse every time it repeated. We were there to determine my fate in that first-round series against our most recent rivals—and, potentially, with the only franchise I'd played for throughout my near decade in the NHL.

But we were also there on account of the past—my history, as the league framed it.

Step out of this crowded, oversuited room for a moment and let's take a look at the factors that earned me that trip to New York.

A YEAR EARLIER, WE MET the Boston Bruins in the first round of the Stanley Cup playoffs. We'd finished fourth in the Eastern Conference, with forty-nine wins—a franchise record for wins in a regular season. The Leafs' new era was supposed to be entering a win-now mode. I was twenty-seven years old and an essential piece, playing the middle on our top two lines. We had tons of talent up front with Matthews, Marner, Nylander, van Riemsdyk, and me. I was now the longest-serving Leaf in the lineup, and one of the few who'd been on the roster during our 2013 collapse in the third period of Game 7. That loss still lingered in my memory.

In Game 1 of that series against Boston in the 2018 playoffs, I wanted to make sure the Bruins knew that our team wasn't going to be pushed around. As we trailed 4–1 in the third, Marner was first hit by Zdeno Chára along the boards and then elbowed in the head by Tommy Wingels. I was at the top of the circle when Wingels hit Mitch with that cheap shot, a bullshit play on one of our best players. It should have been a call. Within a second I was on him. My purpose was to send a message. But just as I went to hammer Wingels into the boards, he fell to his knees. So instead of connecting with his shoulder, I spun as he fell and my hip connected with his head.

It wasn't my intention to hit Wingels like that. And in no way did I mean to hurt him. It was just one of those things that happen in a fast-paced game. If you watched the replay you'd see me turn at the last moment as I see Wingels fall. But I was already airborne. There was nothing I could do.

Still, it was an awkward, ugly play. Wingels went down as soon as I hit him and struggled to get back to his feet.

Chára was on me right after the hit. I'll admit I was nervous, thinking I'd have to fight the big man, but before he could seek retribution, I was mercifully escorted to the box as the familiar "boos" from the Bruins fans rained down.

Honestly, hurting Wingels never once crossed my mind. I just wanted to make my presence known, to say "Hey, you can't take liberties on one of my teammates without paying a price." Most players would do the same. But with my multiple previous infractions I was already on thin ice with the Department of Player Safety.

Nor had there been any thought to hurt a guy in any of my other suspensions. Not once. I don't care if people believe it or not. I do regret the way I approached the hit on Wingels. I should have tried to hold up. But everything happens in the blink of an eye. In my mind he was going to turn into me, I was going to lay a big hit, and then we'd move on. That's what I was thinking.

It worked out differently.

I was playing well in that game. That's what hurts the most, knowing I could have had an impact.

I was handed a three-game suspension for the hit, which took me out for Games 2, 3, and 4. The hit was certainly worthy of a suspension, but three games was a bit hard. All I could do was sit on the sidelines and let my playoff beard grow, trying to stay ready to get back on the ice. I'd had an important role in shutting down the Bruins' top line while adding an offensive threat. I was much more effective being on the ice than I was watching from the box. So I was more pissed at myself than anyone else could have been.

I returned for Game 5 in Boston, with the Bruins holding a 3–1 series lead.

We fought back, barely surviving Game 5 and then playing as well as we knew we could at home in Game 6, winning 3–1 to force another Game 7 against Boston. We'd shown a ton of courage and resilience to get to that point. There was a lot to be proud of, regardless of the outcome. But in that moment, there was only one outcome that interested us.

Given our history, it was as hyped an elimination game as you'll get in the NHL. It was also a wild back-and-forth; we held three leads over its duration and were ahead 4–3 entering the third period.

Then it all fell apart again. The Bruins scored four times in the third period to finish us off for good.

The loss stung, as they always did. But each playoff exit hurt more than the last. This was the third first-round exit I'd been part of as a Leaf and it felt worse than the others, mostly because I'd taken myself out of three games in which I believe I could have made a significant difference. I wasn't going to put all the blame for losing the series on myself—something I've struggled with at times. But it certainly hurt.

A few days later Lou was relieved of his duties as our general manager. It was framed as a plan that had already been in place, but since we'd failed to get out of the first round, it felt like a dismissal.

As we grappled with that early exit, it was apparent that Lou's departure was part of the necessary sacrifice that always follows another disappointing end. That summer we lost Bozak, van Riemsdyk, and Leo Komarov to free agency, which left me as the longest-tenured player on the team and the only one who'd lived through the 2013 collapse against the Bruins. It was tough to see some good buddies move on.

But in that summer of 2018, Kyle Dubas—who replaced Lou as general manager—made a huge move by signing John Tavares. It was an enormous signing for us and a great storyline, as Johnny would be coming home to play for the team he'd grown up watching. I was happy to be reunited with my old Knights teammate. With the addition of Tavares, our team looked to be all in on making another push for the playoffs in the 2018–2019 season.

And it worked. We finished fifth in the Eastern Conference, with forty-six wins—just a few off our record pace the previous year. Johnny led the team with forty-seven goals; Mitch led the team in points with ninety-four; and Matthews put up similar per game numbers but missed time because of an injury. Freddy Andersen put up thirty-six wins for us in goal. And once again, we met the Bruins in the first round of the playoffs.

And what happened in Game 2 of that round is how I ended up in New York, with my future at the mercy of the suits.

Again, I'd stood up for a teammate. And again, it was a hit that looked worse than I'd intended.

WE PLAYED THE FIRST TWO games in Boston, and won the critical first—which meant we'd head back to Toronto with at least a split on the road, if not a two-game lead. But in Game 2, with just over five minutes to go in the third period, we were trailing 3–1.

That's when Patrick Marleau carried the puck into the Bruins' zone and was hit into the stanchion at the Boston bench by Jake DeBrusk. I saw Marleau go down awkwardly. It looked like an aggressive hit by DeBrusk, trying to pin him against the post.

Once again, I reacted right away. As DeBrusk continued into the corner, I tried to give him a cross-check to the chest, but he kind of ducked down as I hit him. My stick bounced up his chest and caught him right in the face. It was completely unintentional. My stick slid up his arm, but I knew the league wouldn't care. DeBrusk would play the next day, so thankfully I hadn't hurt him badly, although he sold it for all it was worth on the ice.

After the hit all hell broke loose. Once again, Chára was on top of me. TD Garden wanted my blood. I was kicked out of the game with a match penalty right away. As soon as I saw the ref gesture, I knew I was fucked and regretted what I'd done. I'd let my emotions get out of check in a game we were still in. And now, with only a few minutes to go, I'd taken us pretty much right out of it. I'd also set myself up to miss more time. It felt like a terrible case of déjà vu.

The next day, Brendan Shanahan told me to pack my bags. We'd been summoned to headquarters for an in-person hearing.

My other hearings had been over the phone, so this didn't bode well for me. In-person hearings were usually reserved for serious cases, and could result in a suspension of five games or more. That's a critical number of games to miss in the playoffs.

The night before the meeting Shanahan and I had dinner in Manhattan at a nice Italian place. We went over what was going to happen the next morning, preparing for it like a court case. I was so anxious I could hardly eat. But Shanahan was supportive. I think he knew what kind of guy I was; he understood my character. He also understood what I'd been trying to do on the play, even though I'd messed up.

At the hotel that night I stayed up late organizing my notes, feeling as if I were about to go on the stand.

SO THERE I WAS THE next morning, over coffee and pastries, surrounded by suits watching the biggest mistake of my career play over and over again. It was a sold-out crowd. Every seat was taken.

It was the most painful thing I'd ever had to sit through.

Everyone was looking at me, then looking at the TV, looking at me, the TV, me, TV, me—frame by frame, in slow motion, over and over—as I screwed myself out of the playoffs and likely my time in Toronto. They played it for probably an hour straight.

And they asked me every question you can think of.

What do you think about the hit?

What were your intentions?

What was your thought process?

They wanted details. It was a full-blown interrogation.

I tried to be as sincere and genuine as possible. I just spoke right from the heart. In doing that, in telling the truth, I felt I was best suited to think on my toes when asked any question, to tell them exactly what I thought. I had nothing to hide.

I wasn't trying to be malicious and hurt anybody. But in hockey, sometimes you have to send a message. In reality, yes, I wanted to get him because of what he did to Patty. I'm thinking that—but I'm not thinking that I wanted to run his face through the dashboard. I'm just trying to get a good lick on him. Knock him down, then maybe drop the gloves and square it away.

Still, I had to be careful, because the disciplinary team could try to twist your words. Like any lawyer, they could take anything you said out of context: "Oh, so it was retaliatory? You were trying to get him back?"

It becomes a bit of a slippery slope.

I was coached before the meeting on how to answer—on things I should say or refrain from saying. I was advised not to mention certain words. A lot of it wasn't so much what you say but how you say it. Everyone knew I was reacting to DeBrusk's hit on Marleau.

But I couldn't say that, because then it becomes retaliatory. I had to be careful not to implicate myself by making it seem premeditated.

That's what made me nervous. I wanted to tell the truth, and yet I didn't want to say it the wrong way.

But every time I spoke it seemed as though I'd made another mistake. By then my dress shirt was drenched. Meanwhile the hit kept playing, frame by frame. And again, the more I watched it, the worse it seemed.

"Holy shit," I thought. "I don't think this is going to be good."

20
FINDING OUT
THE HARD WAY

I SAT IN THE PRESS box in Toronto, watching Game 3 against the Bruins and feeling surprisingly hopeful. We'd just flown back to the city in time to reach Scotiabank Arena by puck drop.

Well before the hearing I'd been convinced that the league had their minds made up. It would all be theatre—a logistical process they had to go through. They'd be watching my sins in slow motion and throwing the book at me before I even walked through those doors.

I'd tried to prepare myself for the worst so that anything less would seem positive. And considering what I'd anticipated, I was okay with the league's ruling. Before we left New York I was told I was suspended for the remainder of the series against Boston. I'd never heard of anything like that before: not a set number of games, just the Boston series. Apparently they thought that if I went up against the Bruins again something crazy was going to happen.

But if we moved on to the second round, I'd be back in the lineup. The series was tied at one game apiece at the time. So if we swept the rest of the series there was a chance I'd be out for just three games. I was being overly optimistic, of course. Boston had a very good team, so we were unlikely to win three in a row.

It was painful to sit in the press box and watch the boys play without me. The first game wasn't so bad. We took it 3–2—potentially reducing my suspension to two more games. I was sure I was going to be back. I was around the guys, practising and everything, trying to stay ready in anticipation of returning.

When we lost the next game 6–4, I felt a little more anxious.

"Oh, shit, I don't know," I thought.

We were knotted at two games each, with the series swinging back to Boston for Game 5. I'd have to stay home; worried about my welfare, they wouldn't allow me to go. There were Wanted posters with my face on them all over the city; Bruins fans were hungering for my head. Since this was the second time I'd been suspended for a hit in Boston, I understood the vitriol.

It was an incredible playoff series. I'm sure the fans enjoyed every minute. For me, though, watching from home, it was brutal. That was the worst part of the punishment.

We took Game 5, 2–1.

The longer the series went, the more anxious I became.

The series returned to Toronto for Game 6. All we needed was one more win to finally get the Bruins off our back and put this whole mess behind us. I did my best to weather the storm, praying we could get over the hump and have another opportunity to play. I just wanted a chance to redeem myself. So I kept practising and preparing, staying ready behind the scenes, making sure I was good to go.

BUT FIRST WE HAD TO get out of the series. I felt sick about not being able to help the guys when they needed me. I was a big part of the team, and so I couldn't help thinking I'd let a lot of people down. It's not like I'm Wayne Gretzky or anything, but as I've said, I knew I'd be more effective on the ice than off.

I also knew that some fans were furious with me. And with a debate going on over what my future with the team should be, I did my best to drown out all the noise. I spoke with my friends and family, but that was pretty much it. I avoided people.

My teammates were great through it all. They could tell I was stressed out by the whole situation, that I cared, that I wanted to win just as much as anybody else. They also knew my hit hadn't come from a selfish place, that I'd reacted to something that had happened to a teammate.

I was as nervous as I'd ever been as I watched Game 6 from the press box. The Bruins extended my purgatory with a 4–2 win— forcing a Game 7.

My punishment had now extended to its fullest length, the agony increasing with each game in the series.

Game 7. And I couldn't even be in Boston.

Fuck me.

I'm a relatively composed guy, but I was an absolute mess for that final game. Sitting alone in my apartment to watch it, I experienced a complete, crippling anxiety about the outcome because I had no control over it. It's funny how when you're actually playing in the game, you don't feel an ounce of that. And again, the worst part about it was feeling that I could have made a difference.

We lost 5–1.

I sat quietly in the corner of my living room, utterly defeated. It was one of the worst days of my life.

That series and the aftermath were easily the hardest times in my career. I let people down, and that's something that haunts me to this day.

I DIDN'T KNOW IT IN the days that followed, but the hit on Tommy Wingels marked my last play in a Maple Leafs uniform. That was how almost a decade with the franchise ended.

A few days after the Game 7 loss I joined the rest of the guys to clear out our stuff for another off-season. It was a terrible feeling. None of us knew what would happen with the team. We'd battled hard, but it wasn't enough. So once again, we knew that changes were inevitable.

Were they planning to get rid of me or not? I was super worried. I didn't want to go anywhere. I wanted to stay with the team.

About a week after we'd been eliminated, I met with the front office and coaching staff. It was a bit of a choppy encounter. They talked about the suspension, and about what they expected from me in the next season. We touched on how the year had gone and what they wanted to see me improve.

I didn't feel great leaving that meeting, but at least we'd hashed it out. Later, I was sent a long message that said, in effect, "You're part of this team, you're part of the future. Let's get to work here."

What a relief. I believed I was okay and was so excited about that—motivated to come back better than ever, determined not to let these guys down again.

Then, in late June, I began receiving calls and texts from people in the Calgary Flames organization trying to convince me to join the team. That was how I learned I was being shopped. No one from the team had said anything about it.

The Leafs confirmed that a deal was in place, but that I had final say over whether it went through or not. My contract included a limited no-move clause, meaning I could nix a trade to any team on a list of about a dozen or so.

Having been told I was part of what we were building in Toronto, I was confused. I'd begun with the Leafs when they were at the bottom, and now we were an up-and-coming contender; I'd started to believe we could get it done, and that's what I intended to do. I loved the team, I loved the city, and I wanted to be part of history there.

It wasn't anything against Calgary. I liked the direction in which they were heading. But Toronto was my home. So I told my agent to reject the deal, feeling like Leonardo DiCaprio in *The Wolf of Wall Street* when he refuses to step down from his company: "I'm not fucking leaving!"

The reality, though, was that the team was trying to get rid of me, whether I wanted to admit it or not. My agent told me there was a fifty-fifty chance I was on the way out. That's when it really sank in.

Word got out quickly. Rumours were going around left, right, and centre. The boys were messaging me, asking me what was going on, urging me to tell them it wasn't true and that I wasn't going anywhere. I tried to reassure them. From what I knew, I was good.

I felt betrayed.

If I'd just been told "Hey, we're shopping you," I would have understood. If I knew they were looking for a better option, it would have hurt and I would have been pissed off, but at least I wouldn't have been blindsided; I would have found peace with it.

To this day, I believe that if Lou had still been the Leafs' general manager I wouldn't have been in that position. I got it to a certain extent. Kyle Dubas had his guys, and I wasn't one of them; I had no connection to him, despite having played in the minors with the Toronto Marlies, where he'd been GM, and against Sault Ste. Marie, where he'd run the OHL's Greyhounds. Still, I'd survived earlier changes in both management and coaching. By now I'd been with the Leafs for nearly a decade and had outlasted all those guys.

I was also stressed out that June because my wife, Ashley, was due to have our first kid in a few days. It was an overwhelming time.

ON JULY 1, THE FIRST day of NHL free agency, I got the call from my agent.

I'd been traded to the Colorado Avalanche for defenceman Tyson Barrie, winger Alex Kerfoot, and a sixth-round selection in the 2020 NHL draft. The Leafs also sent defenceman Calle Rosen and a third-rounder in the deal.

I was the longest-serving Leaf on the roster. Over my entire NHL career I'd given everything I had to that team. Every night I'd played as hard as I could. I'd been there through some of the most difficult times in the team's recent history and had helped us reach a new era of possibility.

And now, just like that, it was over.

I felt sick. It was a lot to deal with at that time—an absolute grind to get through mentally, devastated as I was about the move.

The day after the trade I remember walking through the mall, just going about my business. A guy recognized me and came over to say how angry he was about the trade.

"I couldn't even go to work," he told me. "I had to call in sick I was so upset."

Leafs fans, man.

"Holy shit," I said. "That's crazy."

He was a grown-ass guy who probably shouldn't have been skipping work on account of a player getting traded. But still—that random guy made me feel so good in that moment.

"I really appreciate that," I told him, shaking his hand. "Thank you."

I'd felt as if everything we'd done in Toronto was a waste, but he made me consider things differently. He cheered me up. Maybe I had left some sort of legacy, or some sort of impact, on the city. Maybe people had recognized how hard I'd played.

A few days later I was in a hospital room in Toronto welcoming my first child into the world. The timing alone was a blessing, since it took my mind off hockey and everything going on. I just settled in and enjoyed the first moments of life with my wife and the young family we'd started.

Looking into my baby's beautiful eyes, I realized that so many great things lay ahead for us. The journey was just beginning—and we were heading to the mountains.

21
NEW BEGINNINGS

COLORADO MADE IT VERY EASY to move on. When you answer your phone and Joe Sakic is on the line welcoming you to his team, you quickly forget about the bitterness of being traded unexpectedly. Having an absolute legend at the helm of a team makes you confident about its championship pedigree. Joe told me how much I would love Denver, but to be honest, in the summer of 2019 I didn't need much convincing.

I left behind some incredibly talented teammates in Toronto, but I'd done what I could to stay with them, using my no-trade clause to nix a deal to Calgary. But Colorado wasn't on my no-move list, so I had no say in what happened. As far as forced destinations go, Colorado was as good as it gets.

After speaking with Joe and several of my friends on the team, I did a complete one-eighty. I was all in on Colorado, with a chip on my shoulder because of how things had ended in Toronto. I was ready to get to Denver with my family and move forward. Ashley and I moved with our baby girl to a house with a stunning view of the Rockies. It was an amazing place to live. It felt much more relaxed than Toronto. And the vibes around the club were so positive. There was much less media, but the fanbase was still passionate and knowledgeable.

Vegas bookies were giving us great odds that fall to win it all. I did too. The Avalanche was absolutely stacked. In training camp the locker room was crowded with a group of established vets and young talent. There was Nathan MacKinnon, Gabriel Landeskog, Mikko Rantanen, and a rookie defenceman named Cale Makar. They looked ready-made to win a Stanley Cup. *We* looked ready. I didn't see how any team could stop us.

I'd known MacKinnon for several years, since we'd played together at the 2014 IIHF World Championships. And Landeskog had played for the Kitchener Rangers while I was with London, and we'd also known each other for years. Dion was the clear leader on that Leafs team. There was no question who should be wearing the "C." Gabe set the tone in Denver in the same way. He didn't shy away from having a good time, but he would still show up and be a professional. I think that's what good leaders do. When there's a big game, or a big play to be made, these guys are usually the guys that come through. They can be counted on when their team needs them the most. The best form of leadership is going out there and showing up. They all played a significant role in allowing me to feel comfortable and a part of the group right away. Even though it was the first time I'd played with a new franchise in my career, my transition to the team was seamless. That fall, it immediately felt like I'd been in Colorado longer than I had been. There were a few other new guys that joined that season, which made it easier to fit in. Everybody fit in. We had good chemistry off the ice, and I think that translated to a lot of our on-ice success.

It went beyond the players, too. The families had a connection. The players' girlfriends, wives, and children were all very close. We were like one family unit. Everyone was on the same page. It was drama-free and we enjoyed each other's company. That makes a big difference. It allows you to go out and focus on exactly what you need to accomplish. When these big games come, every single ounce of your energy goes into preparing for and playing these games. It certainly makes a difference when you have guys you trust and respect around you. You can count on them to back you up and you'll back them up. That's key. Maybe that sounds like a small thing— you'd think professional players would just go out and execute. That's their job, right?

But it's almost never that simple. There is usually some kind of tension, whether it's with the head office or the coaching staff. You see that bubble up when things don't go well. But there can also be resentment or jealousy between teammates. Not everyone likes to see a teammate do well, not if it takes away that guy's spotlight, or makes him expendable, or makes his next contract harder to negotiate or whatever. Maybe one guy doesn't like another. Maybe *no one* likes one guy. Some people are just harder to get along with than others. Even families have their black sheep. But that group didn't have any black sheep.

After just a few months with the club, I understood that Colorado had a winning culture. We lived up to the pre-season hype, battling for the top spot in the Western Conference through the fall. I got off to a great start that season centring the second line, and had put up twelve goals and eleven assists by the end of the decade. Nate was putting on a case for the Hart Trophy, with twenty-two goals and thirty-four assists heading into 2020. Makar was running away with the Calder, but he was also generating buzz as a potential Norris Trophy winner. But you don't need stats or journalists' votes to know these two guys were special. MacKinnon's wheels and finish are maybe the most lethal in the game. Makar can take over the game without even looking as though he was trying. They didn't dominate every shift. No one can, and no one does. But you knew that pretty much anything could happen when those two were on the ice.

I knew this was a special opportunity in my career and I didn't take it for granted. Having Joe Sakic around the rink every day was something else. Talking to him casually and picking his brain. He's such an easygoing guy. He'd always given me little pointers too, just little things on the ice. It was surreal to be chatting with a legend who I grew up watching. I still remember when Burnaby Joe was one of Team Canada's specialists at the Olympics. It's safe to say that I always took his advice.

THROUGH MY CAREER I'VE HAD the privilege of playing with some of the best players in the game. In Toronto, I watched guys like Mitch Marner, William Nylander, and Auston Matthews become absolute studs. They were pretty easygoing guys, which is kind of how you have to be in a market like Toronto. They take a lot of unnecessary heat and they take it like champs. I've had the opportunity to see them enter the league and grow as players. They've evolved as players and people. They are always going to be elite players that can drive an entire team. And they are great people too. I'm always cheering for them

In Colorado, I witnessed similar greatness in Cale Makar and Nate MacKinnon—two guys who are very different but share similar qualities as a couple of the best players we've ever seen play the game.

Playing with Cale was an absolute treat. He's an awesome guy. He was a Calgary-born kid and I think that's why he's such a good human being. He was raised very well by an amazing family. It's so nice to play with guys like him who can just give you the opportunity to do what you excel at as a player. Cale was able to facilitate and distribute the puck and allow his teammates to make plays as well as anybody I've seen in the game. He has this quiet confidence— like a muted swagger. He's a very humble kid. But you know that deep down inside, he's a dog.

The league has changed since I first started. I was kind of shunned for being confident in myself. As a veteran guy now, I think players have to earn respect. But I still love to see a young player come in and be confident—borderline cocky, even. I love it when a young player believes in himself.

Of course there are certain rules you need to abide by. There is a hierarchy in the dressing room, and players need to respect that. But as long as you stay in that lane and have respect for the older players, you're good. Believing in yourself is different. That's how you play the game and that's how you carry yourself.

If you're the team's first pick in the draft, I want to see that you believe in yourself. If I'm running a team and I just invested a shit-load of money into a guy, I want him to think he's the best player on the ice all the time. I came up in the transition phase, where you had to work your way up from the American League, regardless of your ability. Nowadays, young players have been put in a position to show what they can do much earlier than when I started. It's become a younger league all around, really.

It helps, of course, if you're as talented as Cale Makar.

But even if you're not, I have a better chance of believing in someone if I know that they believe in themselves. That's rule number one. As a player I've always had respect for those who came before me, but on the ice I didn't care who you were. I'd go out and try to bust your ass. I didn't care if I was standing across from Wayne Gretzky. I was going to try to challenge you and not make it easy on you. That was always the mentality that I had. Sometimes you get humbled very quickly, but most of the time, if you're confident, you can manifest success, and I think it'll work out for you in the end.

There were times when I got burned in my matchup and just got outplayed by the guy that was across from me. But I never let that discourage me. I was never the kind of guy to point fingers and blame everybody else. I was always able to look in the mirror and reflect on what I could do to make sure that didn't happen again. If you have that kind of pride, it will take you a long way. You don't want to be humiliated. You want to pull through for your team. At the end of the day, you have to understand how you can get better and the changes you can make to get there.

Nate always had that kind of confidence. As a generational player, his confidence is much louder than Cale's. He has an elite swagger. They call him The Dogg for a reason. He is one. Nate and I would "mother-fuck" each other all the time. We'd see a play a little differently and we'd let each other know the way that hockey players do. We'd mouth-off to each other on the bench or in the dressing room between periods. We'd tear each other apart. And then when the game ended, we'd go out for dinner like nothing happened. Sometimes we'd even laugh about it.

We got along very well. We're both ruthless competitors. We did whatever it took to win. Nate is also one of the most special players I've ever seen. That's why he's had the success that he's had. You look at the things he's doing and it's absolutely remarkable. He holds his teammates accountable, but he's doing it all. Whatever he says, he's doing. You have to follow his lead.

It wasn't always rosy though. It shouldn't be. We were a competitive group with big expectations about what we could accomplish. We were all on the same page there, but that also meant that there would inevitably be conflict. There always is an environment set on winning.

Our coach Jared Bednar and I had our challenges. We were both competitive guys who wanted to see the team succeed. In the heat of the moment, we had some arguments. But we respected each other, and we were able to set aside our differences in the end. At the heart of our conflict, we both knew that we had the same goal.

It was the same with guys on the team. When you have a group of ultra-competitive people, there are going to be disagreements and frustration will boil over. That's inevitable. It's bizarre, but that's how it works. That's the kind of relationship you need with your teammates to be successful.

I'm often asked what makes the difference between a good team and a team that can win a championship. Is there a difference in how a team that wins a title meshes on and off the ice together?

I think what I found in Colorado was a key element.

There is going to be adversity over the course of a season, especially when you're on course to compete for a championship. There are going to be games where guys lose their composure and go after each other. But it was something that none of us ever took personally. As soon as the game finished, we were back to normal, with everything behind us.

The focus has to be on pushing each other to be better for the sake of the team.

As a competitor, you can't be overly sensitive. That's something I've had to learn as I've grown and evolved as a player.

Fighting through hard times decides whether you will make it or not.

Over the years I've been through a lot of internal battles, the kind of stuff that every player is going to go through at some point.

You go from peak stardom with your junior team, at seventeen or eighteen years old, and a lot can change over the next decade, by the time you're in your late twenties.

I've had to learn not to take things personally. That's difficult for a lot of people. It was difficult for me when I was younger, but with time I learned to not let the noise get to me.

Some people can get overly sensitive about things. That's not to say that there is anything wrong with sensitivity. But there is value in having the memory of a goldfish.

Whether something great happens or something terrible happens, tomorrow is a new day. I've learned to wake up and focus on tackling every day in a way that will make me better than I was the day before. When you face difficulties, you can't just hang your head, dwell on it, and let it affect your confidence. That's how you let it defeat you.

That's easier said than done, of course. And there are obviously degrees of hardship that you can't simply tough your way through.

But when you start to let criticism get to you, that goldfish mentality becomes a difference maker.

If you throw a pizza up the middle and turn it over in a playoff game, and someone comes down and scores the game-winning goal off your turnover—yeah, it's a huge mistake, but are you going to be anxious and scared for the rest of your career? Or are you going to say, "Okay, that sucked, but now I have to be prepared"—and then get back out there.

I've seen criticism affect a lot of people differently over the years. I've played with some people who don't react very well to it, and some people who let it roll off their back like water.

I think that's an important message: If you dwell on your mistakes or let critique get to you personally, it ends up compounding and becoming a bigger distraction. You get stuck in a cycle where you're not capable of playing the way you know you can. You let that define you. There are always going to be holes that we fall in. That's inevitable—in professional sports, but also life in general. There are always going to be points in our life where we find ourselves in a rut. What makes a difference is having that confident mentality, that mental toughness, to overcome it. Throughout my career I've noticed that the best players are able to quickly pull themselves out of their low moments. Bad days will happen, but the key to success is how you respond to them.

Of course, some guys might react differently than others. As a teammate and a leader, you have to be aware of who you are speaking to and respect your teammates' personalities. The idea is to be a cohesive unit, and you're never going to do that if you don't have a sense of who your teammates are and how they will respond in different scenarios.

MY FIRST SEASON WITH AVALANCHE was going as well as I could have hoped. But in March 2020, the world was derailed by COVID-19 and the season was suddenly shut down. It was a bit of a bizarre way to start with a new team, but being in Avalanche through it all was a silver lining. From my perspective, being traded to Colorado was the best thing that could have happened to me at the time. Instead of being locked down in a large city like Toronto, I was in the mountains in

Denver. The weather was great and the city was never really 100 percent shut down like Toronto was. You could still eat on a patio and enjoy the outdoors. And we had a large house, which gave us a lot more room than a condo in Toronto. We barbequed outside pretty much every day, surrounded by the mountains. The spring weather was incredible.

Most importantly, I was able to spend some quality time with my wife and daughter during the shutdown. It was time with my baby that I wouldn't have otherwise had. The forced period away from the frantic pace of an NHL career allowed me to slow down and enjoy those moments as my daughter neared her first birthday.

And we had a large house, which gave us a lot more room than a condo in Toronto. We barbequed outside pretty much every day, surrounded by the mountains. The spring weather was incredible.

I don't mean to diminish the real hardships that people endured through the pandemic. But for us, it was an opportunity to put life into a clearer perspective. The game consumed so much of my time and attention. I'm as passionate about the game as anyone. But I loved being a father more than anything, and having the chance to just stop and enjoy this time with my young family was a blessing for me.

But those were not times that everyone will remember as a blessing. There were protests occurring across the United States and in Canada, particularly in response to police violence against Black people following the murder of George Floyd by a white police officer in Minneapolis. Cities were in flames. Everyone could see that something was very wrong with our society. There were difficult conversations happening about racism, many of them very angry.

Those months away from hockey gave me some room to reflect on my place in the game as one of the few non-white players in the league. I wasn't the only one. At the time, several of my NHL colleagues were already meeting regularly by Zoom to discuss racism in the game. We wanted to start a group focused on eradicating the prejudice that still exists at all levels of the game, including youth hockey and junior hockey. Our experiences were all different, but similar.

Earlier that season, Akim Aliu had gone public with the bigotry he experienced playing elite level hockey growing up and while playing for an AHL team. By sharing his story, Akim spearheaded a reckoning in the sport. He was one of the driving forces behind establishing the group.

For obvious reasons, racism and stereotyping in sport has always been a sensitive subject for me. I'd dealt with it pretty much my entire life, being called vulgar names and phrases since I was young. The complexion of my skin, my family's Lebanese heritage, and my Muslim faith made me a target in a sport that is played by a majority of white players.

As I grew up, I started to think that maybe prejudice was starting to fizzle out of the game. It seemed like people were a little bit smarter than they'd been before. It became less acceptable to say those kinds of things publicly. People were being held more accountable than they had been in decades before.

But I've since realized that just because expressing hate becomes more taboo, doesn't mean the ideas themselves are eradicated. These people still exist, they've just become more closeted. As a pro in the age of social media, it quickly becomes apparent what people are capable of when they are able to hide beneath the cloak of anonymity.

They knew exactly what they were saying. The comments about me being Brown. And comments about me being a Muslim hockey player that were way off base. People were taking shots intentionally. They weren't just getting pissed off and spouting a bunch of bullshit. This was clearly something that was on their mind.

As I described earlier, it was particularly bad when I was younger.

I remember hearing it first when I was probably ten or eleven years old, right to my face. These people were open and aggressive about who they were.

And it started at the rink. That's where I heard most of it. You really get to find out who somebody is when they are put in that kind of an atmosphere and the competitive juices are flowing. Sometimes people get a little too rambunctious and they say something that they don't necessarily want to say, but it's something that is in them.

It sucks to be a kid and to hear things like that said to you. It's something that I was very confused about and didn't know how to react to. It made me feel self-conscious and vulnerable. Luckily, I had a great family who had my back through anything. I leaned on my parents and my sisters whenever I faced something like that.

I feel bad for people who are poisoned by that kind of mindset. You'd hear parents saying that shit, and you can only imagine how their kids are going to turn out. When I'd hear it from other players, I'd know that it was something they were hearing at home. No one is born with hate in their heart. It's something you learn.

It's something that pisses me off when I still see it happening in our game or beyond it. From my standpoint, I felt it was my responsibility to share my experiences and use whatever influence I have to help kids who are facing something similar today.

As our group met over Zoom, talking for hours and hours, we realized that we had an opportunity to make a difference, to help future generations of marginalized children fall in love with the game—and feel welcome in it. We all knew that there was a need. We knew that it was finally time to make these conversations more widespread. It was an exciting time. We connected with potential partners and sponsors, just trying to figure out where we could take this.

I'm proud to say that I became a co-founding member of the Hockey Diversity Alliance, along with Aliu, Trevor Daley, Matt Dumba, Anthony Duclair, Wayne Simmonds, Chris Stewart, and Joel Ward. It was born out of our meetings to make a difference in the game at all levels. We've raised significant funds, working alongside some very big-name sponsors, like Kraft Heinz, Budweiser, Canadian Tire, Scotiabank, and CCM. It's become a literal game changer. We've started grassroots development ice and ball hockey programs to engage and support children in underserved communities. We've created educational programming to help foster an ongoing dialogue about racism and discrimination in hockey at all levels. And we've continued to develop extracurricular programs, scholarships, and mentorships to help support and inspire participation in the game.

As we eventually got back on the ice and went back to the frantic pace of NHL life amid the ongoing pandemic, I was happy to see that the hockey community responded well to our initiatives. We had support from our teammates and many fans. I felt encouraged about where the topic of racism in hockey was heading.

What none of us could know was that the kind of hate my colleagues and I were trying to stamp out would flare up far away from any NHL rink, and much closer to home for me.

On June 6, 2021, a man in London, Ontario, drove a pickup truck into a family as they were out for an evening walk together. It was an unthinkable, horrific attack. The man targeted the family because of their Muslim faith. Two of the victims wore traditional Pakistani clothing. The man saw the family—a grandmother, father, mother, and their two children—standing on the sidewalk waiting for the light to turn. He did a U-turn and purposefully accelerated right into them. Four members of the family were killed. Only the family's nine-year-old son survived.

It was heartbreaking. Such a cowardly act of hate, attacking an innocent family. Not all that unlike my family. Like everyone in Canada, I was shaken. But it was particularly hard to process that the family had been targeted because of their faith. That hit close to home in more ways than one.

As a member of the Muslim community in London, I was asked for my reaction to the vile tragedy. What do you say? There really are no words to properly address that kind of heinous act, the enormity of the loss that the community is left to grapple with. I typed out my best effort on Twitter, which shared a hope that seemed difficult to cling to in the aftermath.

"Will continue to conquer racism together . . . May love always be stronger than hate."

The animosity that emerged out of the attack in London put a lot into perspective for me. That summer, I thought a lot about my family's journey—about how I'd been given the opportunity to live a dream, thanks to the sacrifices of my parents and their parents, who came to Canada to make this country their home. I knew how hard they had worked so that I could find my way to this point in a career that none of us could really imagine. I thought about my grandfather, working those jobs just to take care of his family. I couldn't imagine how someone could despise a man like that, just because of his race and his faith.

It was crushing to think that it didn't matter what kind of character you had, what kind of work you put in, what kind of person you were—there would always be people out there who'd look at you and feel blind hatred.

22
WHERE IT ALL CAME TOGETHER

FOR ME, THE 2022 STANLEY CUP playoffs started in the spring of '21.

I was sitting in the box in St. Louis, my mind spinning. That's when my personal Cup run started. It took over a year for that spinning to stop.

It was Game 2 of the first round of the playoffs. We'd finished first in the Western Conference and won the Presidents' Trophy for the NHL's best team in the regular season. It was shortened to a 56-game season, which was limited to divisional play, as the league tried to find a way back during the pandemic. Nothing was normal, but we were on top of the league and a favourite to win the Stanley Cup.

We'd won the first game of our opening playoff series against the St. Louis Blues.

But now, I was in the box as the Blues' Justin Faulk lay motionless on the ice, as the team's doctor knelt on the ice beside him.

I knew it was bad.

The Blues had been on the attack. Robert Thomas cut in on two defenders in our zone and dropped the puck to Faulk, who'd jumped up from the back end to join the rush. As I backchecked on the left side, I saw the pass and cut across the ice to stop Faulk from taking a well-screened shot on net. I tried to hit him in the chest, but Faulk was in the motion of shooting, leaning forward, as we collided. He didn't see me coming. My shoulder connected with his head. He went down right away. He didn't move for a long time.

I felt sick as I sat in the box. I hoped that Justin would be okay. We play a tough game, but you never want to see another player get seriously hurt.

After a review, the ref gave me a match penalty. I was out for the game. But the issue was far from settled. The league was sure to review the hit.

This time, it was over a Zoom call. Once again, I tried to plead my case. I knew that I hadn't tried to connect with Faulk's head, but the intent didn't matter. The video evidence was there and my past suspensions meant that the league was going to throw the book at me.

They gave me eight games, which feels like a life sentence in the playoffs. We appealed the suspension, but the league upheld it.

I sat out for the remainder of the series against St. Louis, which we swept in four straight games, as headlines and commentary across the hockey world declared that the Leafs had been right to trade me because I was a liability for any team in the playoffs.

I couldn't argue back in that moment. It was the lowest I'd ever felt in my career—even worse than when I watched from the sidelines in Toronto.

How did I get here again?

I knew that I had done this to myself and that I had let my team down when we had a legitimate chance to win the Cup.

During that time, I reflected on a lot of the lessons learned throughout my career. I'd faced a lot of criticism, and for the most part had been able to push through it. But now, it was hard for me to not believe the commentary.

I sat on the sidelines as my teammates battled the Las Vegas Golden Knights in the second round. It was a dogfight of a series, in which I knew I could have contributed. We led the series 3-2 heading into Game 6. It went to overtime, where a single goal for us would have put us through and helped end my nightmare. Vegas scored the winner.

It came down to Game 7, which was the final game of my suspension.

If we won, I'd have been able to rejoin my team for the Stanley Cup semifinals. But Vegas had other ideas. They handed us a 6-3 loss and our season was over.

I felt sick.

In pro sports, there are pressures that are sometimes taken for granted. We have a small window of time—ten to fifteen years, if we're lucky—to live our dream. That's an incredible privilege, of course. But it comes with a lot of pressure. The expectations are ruthless. If you have a bad day at the office, depending on the market, everyone is discussing it. There are a million people watching your games, talking about how you screwed up and how terrible you are. You're under the microscope—your value is dissected piece by piece.

The slightest regression in your ability jeopardizes your livelihood. At this level there is always someone very talented waiting to take your place.

I've had to learn this more times in my career than I can remember.

It affected me a lot more when I was younger. As I got older, my skin got thicker, and I was able to tolerate and shake this stuff off a lot easier. But when I was starting out, it was a big challenge, especially being thrown right into the firepit in Toronto. When everyone has an opinion about you, it's tough to ignore—especially when there are false narratives being spun that are completely made up and untrue. People just roll with it, regardless of the truth. And all you can do is sit back and watch it unfold, because if you respond and give it oxygen, it just gets worse.

I was always very hard on myself. And now I struggled facing this misfortune once again, because it was on a whole other level than what Toronto prepared me for, with all the media and everybody forming their own opinions about you.

I'd lean on my family a lot during that time. I spoke to my old man, my mom, my sisters—they kind of helped me take my mind off things. But it was definitely difficult. It's not easy to shrug off. It's hard to just move forward and not be distracted by it. It's easier said than done.

Even though you might have a "fuck you" attitude, like I've had at times, you start to buy into it a little bit when it gets told to you constantly. It's hard to block out. Luckily, I was able to believe in myself enough to fight through it.

How do you receive it? How do you respond to it? Those are the most important questions. Is it going to ruin you? Because I've seen that happen to a lot of people. But I've also seen the opposite happen, where people thrive on that hardship, and they use it to grow.

I was able to do that.

When I was coming up, Twitter and other social media existed, but it wasn't quite as bad as it has become in the past few years. That's something that the younger guys coming up in the league have had to battle and will continue to battle. It's inevitable that other people are going to be talking about you. You can't control what they say. And you've got to trust yourself and believe in yourself. That's first and foremost.

I'd seen it all.

But at the end of the 2021 season, it felt like everyone had made up their mind about me. I wanted to believe they were wrong. I tried to. For the first time, though, I couldn't shake the feeling that maybe the haters were right about me.

SO IT'S AN UNDERSTATEMENT TO say that I returned to Colorado in the 2021–2022 season with a lot on my mind.

I'd carried the guilt of my suspension the previous spring all season, determined to prove to my teammates—and myself—that I could be relied on. I was on a mission. I was about to enter free agency, so it was a big year for me. I just wanted to leave it all out there on the line. I wasn't sure what the future looked like for me coming into that final season in Colorado. Though I hoped to stay, I didn't know if I would be back in Denver.

I set a new personal best with 28 goals and added 59 assists—putting up more than a point per game for the first time in my career. That season, I must have fought three guys on the Blues to answer for the Faulk incident. I anticipated it and I was ready to face the consequences, as always. Even though I regretted how things unfolded—and if I could take the hit back, I would in a heartbeat—I wasn't hiding from anybody. I said, hey, it is what it is.

I was injured that March, which took me out for eight games, before I returned for the final game of the regular season. It was the first full 82-game season back following the two previous pandemic-affected years. We finished first in the Western Conference and were considered a favourite to win the Cup. There was a unique quality to that team. You knew that you had talented guys around you—guys like Cale, Gabe, Nate, and Mikko. You looked around the room and didn't have to wonder if somebody was going to show up on a nightly basis. These guys were great players, and they were going to do what they do. They were going to be ready to play no matter who we were playing, no matter where we were playing. There was a confidence in the group that we were all going to bring it. And if it was a big game, we were going to bring it even more. We had great veteran guys and young talent. Erik Johnson and Jack Johnson. Andrew Cogliano, who played something like 1,200 games and finally got it done. He was a huge contributor to our run. It was just a good story.

We had the right pieces. And we entered the playoffs in a dominating fashion, knowing that we were one of the best teams in NHL history.

Just before the playoffs started, I got hit with the flu. It was an omen of things to come that spring.

For several days, I laid in bed feeling like I was going to die. My fever hit 105. It was insane. I worried that I wouldn't be able to start our series against the Nashville Predators, but I was determined not to let that happen.

I suited up for the first game of the series, still battling the flu. It was brutal. I felt like shit out there. I spent a couple days back in bed, hoping to be well enough to play the next game. I'd never felt so terrible in my life.

Thankfully we walked over Nashville in four straight games, and I was able to recoup my strength in time for a round two rematch with St. Louis Blues. Given our history, we knew from the start that it would be a rough series.

We split the first two games of the series, which was just as heated as anticipated.

Early in the first period of Game 3, I lunged for a rebound off a shot from Artturi Lehkonen and got tied up with Blues' defenceman Calle Rosen. I was going for the loose puck as Rosen leaned into me. We crashed into Blues goalie Jordan Binnington, who was hurt on the play and had to leave the game. It was unfortunate, but it was a hockey play. After the game, Binnington chucked an empty water bottle at me while I did a live television interview.

The next day after our practice at the Enterprise Center in St. Louis, our media came into the locker room and told me that two cops wanted to see me.

I was baffled.

"Why do they want to see *me*?" I asked.

We arranged to meet them back at the team's hotel. The cops, both undercover, took me into a conference room and pulled out a massive folder of printed material. They told me they had a legal obligation to tell me about the death threats and racist comments that circulated online during and after Game 3.

The stack was thicker than I could stretch my finger to my thumb.

"Do you want to read these?" One of the officers said.

"Are they bad?" I asked.

"They are terrible," he said.

I wanted to see it.

I took the stack and started flipping through the pages.

The comments were the most disgusting things I'd ever heard. They went after my race, my background, and my faith.

It was serious. This wasn't just about a game. This was personal. They went after my family. They threatened my life—they threatened my family members. People actually said that they were going to come and kill me and my family.

There were too many pages to read them all entirely. I'm pretty comfortable in my own skin, which I love about myself. But when people are constantly chipping away, calling you names—and it's very vulgar, disgusting, racially-motivated stuff—it can be overwhelming. I felt like I was going to throw up after they showed me those threats. I've seen some racist shit over the years—people calling me all kinds of names. I've heard it all. But this was a different animal. I'd had two undercover cops in my face saying, "We are legitimately worried about you." With all of the racist nonsense I'd experienced playing the game over the years, I'd never felt so directly in danger before. My family had never been targeted like this. This was worse than anything I'd ever experienced playing the game I loved and dedicated so much of my life to.

The police and the Avalanche rightfully treated the incident like an immediate security threat. They arranged to have a police presence in the hotel, with a couple of officers posted outside of my room. Back in Denver, officers were sent to sit outside of my house, where Ashley and our daughter were.

I skipped dinner. I sat in my hotel room, my head spinning. I was completely in my head about it. I was insecure and self-conscious. I was shaken. I'm not an overly sensitive guy, but was scared for my family back in Denver. How terrifying must it have been for them to see officers posted outside our front door? I wanted to be able to protect them but I couldn't get home. I was halfway across the country.

There wasn't anything anybody could say to me at that moment to help me through it. I just had to persevere mentally. I had to hold it together. I was about to play one of the biggest games of my life, but all I could think about were these threats by unhinged people.

When I woke up the next day, my mentality changed.

I was angry and determined. I was going to shove it in everybody's face. It brought out a hatred in me. Obviously not a hatred as vulgar as their hatred for me, but I felt like I couldn't let them win. I couldn't let them have this one. I'd been through a rollercoaster of emotions over the past day, but now I was steady. I was focused. I was still mad as hell, but I channeled that rage into something useful. My mindset completely flipped. My anxiety turned into adrenaline. I was ready to come out and have the biggest game of my life. I had a swaggy, heated energy.

"Fuck these people," I said. "I'm going to make them pay for this."

I couldn't sleep that afternoon when I tried to take my pre-game nap. I couldn't wait to get on the ice.

"I'm going to score tonight and I'm going to rub it into everyone's face," I thought.

Our bus arrived at the Enterprise Center and we walked off single-file to enter the rink, like we always did. But this time, I was met by officers as soon as I stepped off the bus. It felt like I was going to be whacked. Was someone waiting in the bushes to come stab me? The officers stayed beside me as I walked into the arena and into the dressing room. They hovered around me as I stretched in the hallway. It was full Presidential shit. There was extra security and officers posted around the arena. It was absolutely wild.

The Blues took a 1–0 lead in the first period. We tied it up early in the second on a goal from Erik Johnson.

Just over four minutes into the period, I broke in on a two-on-one with Mikko Rantanen. I knew I was shooting the entire time. I didn't even make it look like a pass was an option. Just past the hash marks,

I fired short-side on Ville Husso, beating him just above his pad. As my teammates rushed to celebrate the goal, I turned to the St. Louis crowd with my hand to my ear as though I was trying to hear them.

The Blues fans were silent.

I wasn't done with them. A few minutes later, I slid into the same spot in the slot—just below the hash marks and the faceoff dot. Bowen Byram took a rebound near the goal line off a Cale Makar shot and fired a perfect pass to me between two Blues defenders. I snapped a one-timer along the ice past Husso's outstretched leg.

The goal put us up 4–1. As I skated back toward my bench, I let out a loud shout and then nodded, to make sure everyone in the building knew what was up.

But I still wasn't done.

The Blues fought back, scoring two to finish up the second, making it a 4–3 game heading into the final period. It remained a one-goal game until halfway through the third, when the Blues failed to clear their zone and I picked up a loose puck near the left faceoff dot. I quickly snapped another low shot on the short side, which caught Husso by surprise. The puck made an audible thud when it hit the padding at the back of the net, completing the hat trick. This time I dipped down and gave the full fist pump celebration as I glided the glass.

I absolutely gave it to them that day. I made sure everybody in St. Louis was aware of who had scored a hat trick. Maybe I should be thanking them for setting me off—but I wasn't in the mood for gratitude. After every goal we scored, the arena was completely silent. Nobody could say shit. The Blues fans looked completely dejected. All they could do was hang their heads.

It was my first playoff hat trick. May 23, 2022. I also added an assist, for good measure. We beat the Blues 6–3. The past 18 hours had been a complete rollercoaster, going from a state of fear and shock, to feeling alone and angry—to triumph. I found a way to persevere through it. I learned a lot about myself in that moment and about the journey I'd been on to that point. In the face of adversity, I stood tall. I was proud. I knew my family was proud. I scored those goals for my wife and our daughter. I scored for my sisters and my mother. For my dad—and for his dad, the original Nazem.

I felt all kinds of swagger. I came for vengeance. I turned that killer instinct. We buried them that night. There was no way the Blues were coming back after we went up three games to one in the series.

It was a pivotal moment in our playoff run.

No one was ever charged for the threats. The police tried to trace a few of the most egregious accounts, but it didn't go anywhere. The worst posts were by anonymous accounts. Of course, they were all a bunch of cowards. That's always how it is. They hide behind their computer screens. But at the end of the day, you don't know what these people are capable of. You have to take it seriously—you don't know how unhinged some people can be, especially when they are capable of saying that kind of shit.

I didn't let it affect me after that. Why would I let these people get the best of me? I felt a sense of pride and confidence that I'd carried throughout my life in hockey, since I was a kid hearing racist insults shouted from the stands. It's traumatic. It took some time to have that mindset. But over the years, I developed a sense of pride in not allowing these kinds of people to dictate how I felt about myself. I conquered their hate. I refused to let them win.

A WEEK LATER, IN THE Western Conference final against the Edmonton Oilers, I was hit from behind by Evander Kane going into the boards full speed. I put my hand out to brace the impact, but I shattered my thumb and some bones in my hand.

I knew it was broken right away. I looked at my hand and I could see the thumb bone was out of place. It was visibly busted. It was a nauseating feeling.

People often think, broken thumb, not that big a deal. But we take for granted how critical our thumb is for our hand to function.

I had to sit with it broken for a couple days, as I returned to Colorado for surgery. I felt sick the entire time. My hand was mangled, and the pain was brutal.

When I finally met the surgeon, he was doubtful about my ability to continue in the playoffs. I'd shattered the base and tip of my thumb.

"It's not looking good for you," he said. "This is probably an eight-to-ten-week recovery."

The Stanley Cup final was a week away.

"Nope," I said. "You're wrong. Give me two weeks."

There I was with zero medical experience, in complete denial of what this doctor was telling me. I was determined not to miss my chance to play for the Stanley Cup.

I went to surgery right away. The surgeon knew that I was going to try to force my way back early, so he said he would reinforce my hand by putting in a few extra pins. The bones in my thumb were held together from the base to the tip. Later, when I was lying on the surgery recovery table, still high as a kite on morphine, I scrolled through Instagram and saw a post that said "Nazem Kadri—Out for the rest of the playoffs."

"Yeah, we'll see . . ." I responded beneath the post.

I have no memory of doing that. My wife showed it to me later.

"Your comment is blowing up," she told me. "It's everywhere."

WHERE IT ALL CAME TOGETHER

"What do you mean?" I said. "What comment?"

I watched as our team played the first three games of the Stanley Cup final against the Tampa Bay Lightning without me. It was terrible. I felt sick watching my team play without me—again.

I was back on the ice three days after surgery, but I couldn't put my hand in my regular glove. I was given a custom, oversized glove because my hand was so swollen. It was huge, like a balloon. I wanted to stay in game shape and keep my conditioning up, but I couldn't even hold my stick, so I went out there and bag skated without one. The next day I would try to put my stick in my hand, but I could still hardly grip it. There was a point where I considered duct taping my stick to my glove so I wouldn't drop it.

With each new day, I put my head down and kept working. Meanwhile, the boys won the first two games at home, but lost Game 3 in Tampa—which was our first loss on the road the entire playoffs. We were a confident team. We felt like we could go into any building and be dominant. It's a pretty wild stat to reach the Stanley Cup finals without having dropped a single game on the road.

By Game 4—as we led 2–1 in the series—I convinced everyone that I was able to return. It was exactly fourteen days after I'd had surgery.

If I'm being honest now, I definitely wasn't ready to come back. My hand was still a mess. I couldn't brush my teeth or wipe my own ass. I needed help putting on my gear and taping my stick. Our trainer had to tie my skates. I was like a six-year-old kid getting ready for a game. Looking back on it, it was absolute insanity. During warmups, I could barely hold onto my stick. I was given a shot before the game to freeze the top half of my thumb. It was painful because the injection was so close to the wrist. And they could only freeze the top half because if they froze the bottom of my thumb, my entire hand would go numb. I couldn't feel a thing near the tip, but the bottom half was swollen and very painful. So I had no feeling on part of my thumb and way too much feeling on the rest of it.

It was impossible to grip the stick properly. It was like my hand was asleep. When I had the puck, I couldn't feel its weight. I must have dropped my stick 10 or 15 times in that game. I obviously wasn't at my best. But I still knew that I could go out there and make a play or two and maybe give us a chance to win.

We went into overtime, tied 2–2. With eight minutes left in the first overtime period, I picked up a stretch pass and broke in on a one-on-three. I cut around Lightning defenceman Mikhail Sergachev and broke in on Andrei Vasilevskiy. I fired a shot under his arm. The puck disappeared. For several moments, no one knew where it was. I circled in the corner, looking back at the net. I thought it was in, but I didn't see the net move or the puck bounce out. I couldn't tell what had happened to it. Vasilevskiy kept his arm down like he had it. No one was reacting. Steven Stamkos saw it first. I saw his reaction when he noticed the puck tucked between the net and the back bar. He tried to poke it out, but by then everyone had already seen it. We went nuts.

I'd scored the biggest goal of my life—an overtime winner in a Stanley Cup final. That little boy shuffling across the ice at Victoria Park all those years ago couldn't have dreamed of anything sweeter. It was a huge win. If we lost that game the series would have been tied. Instead, we went up 3–1 in the series. We knew it wasn't over yet, but we had a stranglehold on the series.

We just needed one more. For me, the challenge was regrouping, because after the overtime win, my hand swelled up like a balloon again. I still couldn't dress myself, among other things, to start Game 5.

We hoped to win it at home, in front of our fans. My parents, sisters, and their families all made the trip to Denver, planning to be there if we won. But Tampa Bay was a veteran team who'd been here before. They weren't about to make anything easy for us. They held on for a 3–2 lead, forcing a must-win Game 6 in Tampa.

We flew to Florida, planning to return with the Cup. My parents made the trip, while the rest of my family gathered at our home in Denver to watch the game. When I woke up the morning of Game 6, the pins in my thumb had punctured out of my bone and ripped through my skin. The team doctor did his best to freeze my thumb, while still allowing me to grip my stick. I had to play through a mix of numbness and excruciating pain. The pins were literally sticking out of my hands that game. But we were so close to reaching the moment I'd dreamed of my entire life.

We played another strong game on the road, leaving no doubt that we were the best team in the world. Stamkos scored first for Tampa, but we answered with goals from MacKinnon and Artturi Lehkonen in the second period. We carried that 2–1 lead into the third. We fought like hell through the final frame to hold on. The closer we got the faster my heart raced.

I watched the final seconds fall off the clock—

Three . . . Two . . . One . . .

Triumph.

In that moment you feel it all, the eruption of all emotion—every agonizing defeat, every thrilling win, every mistake, every game winner, every broken bone, every word of doubt, every racial slur, every time you believed in yourself when it seemed like no one else did. I rushed to my teammates as we celebrated on the ice in Tampa. I was weightless. It was like an out-of-body experience. It was difficult to process what was happening in the moment.

Throughout my entire career, I'd felt like I knew what it would take to reach this moment in the dream. But until you get there, you have no idea. Any player who has won the Cup will understand that. You don't know how hard it is until you do.

I embraced my teammates, guys I'd stood beside and who stood beside me all season, especially through the hardest days. I was so happy to share this moment with them. We'd each battled through hell to get there together. We'd played without Nathan MacKinnon and Gabriel Landeskog through significant stretches through the season, but still found a way to navigate that.

There is no better team sport in the world. And winning a Stanley Cup is one of the toughest grinds in all of sport. You can't get there without the people beside you.

You have to be able to count on each other. You should be able to look around the room and know that everyone around is, without question, going to give it everything they've got and that they are going to be great players as they do. We knew that we could count on each other to bring our best, night in and night out.

I would never have reached this moment without them—and each of those guys would hold a special place in my heart because of it. We completely changed the vibe in Denver. To have such great teammates, such great staff, and such great fans. We went sixteen and four in the playoffs, nine and one on the road. In my opinion, not only were we one of the best teams in the league that year, but we were also one of the best teams of all time. That was how good we were on the ice, but also the type of guys we had on the team.

Having those guys beside me in St. Louis gave me the confidence and strength to play my best, despite the threats. They helped me get through it. Knowing that they were in my corner, and that they would have my back no matter what—that means a lot when you're in a vulnerable situation. You see and support each guy on the team through their own personal journey through the long course of a season. There is something magical in that.

I made it through the handshake line with Tampa using my left hand because my right was a swollen, bloodied mess.

In Colorado, my sisters stood in front of our television, crying and cheering. My parents found their way to the ice—my father celebrating a boyhood dream that had once seemed impossible.

At the end of the line, I was ushered over for a television interview with Sportsnet, riding an overwhelming high of adrenaline and joy.

"It's such a rollercoaster ride," I told Elliotte Friedman and David Amber during the interview. "I couldn't even tie my own skates . . . I don't care, I was going to be out here one way or another."

Amber asked me about all the fans back home in Ontario who had watched me grow—in London and in Toronto—and had supported me through my career.

"I love you guys," I said. "I've had supporters in my corner from day one, never wavered . . ."

I smiled wide, overcome with joy.

"And for everybody who thought I was a liability in the playoffs—you can kiss my ass."

A few moments later, it was my turn to take the Cup. I was worried that I wouldn't be able to lift it over my head. My hand was wrapped up with bandages and was oozing blood. Even with adrenaline coursing through my body, it was still difficult to lift the Cup above my shoulders. I almost dropped it. But I hoisted it as high as I could, looking up at that silver glimmer. It hurt like hell, in the most beautiful way.

23
SHUFFLING ON THE EDGES

I RETURNED TO THE LONDON Muslim Mosque with the Stanley Cup in June 2022. It was a warm day in my hometown and there was excitement everywhere. Hundreds of people, young and old, came to the Mosque to catch a glimpse of the dream that I first carried as a boy, back when my grandfather would bring me, my sisters, and our cousins here every Friday.

At that time, no Muslim-born player had ever won the Stanley Cup. Most children with Middle Eastern ancestry had different dreams, tied to the land of their parents. Hockey was not a sport for Arabs then. At least that's how it seemed. My father had defied that idea. The love he found for a frozen game and passed on to me was the beginning of my crazy journey. But my grandfather's courage to come to a country where he could safely provide and raise his family was the foundation of all of this.

I looked around at all the young people who came to see me and the Cup that day, as we celebrated a moment in history. I tried to imagine what it would have been like for me to see a player who looked like me, who shared my heritage, hoisting the Cup when I was young.

What would that have meant to me? Whose posters would have been on my wall? What confidence would that have given me when people in the stands shouted that I didn't belong in their game?

I don't know. I found my pride in my family. I found the ability to dream of impossible things because I understood the value of hard work and the unyielding power of belief. I knew that nothing could stop me because nothing could stop my father.

I was the first person to bring the Stanley Cup to a mosque in the trophy's 130-year history. But I knew that I wouldn't be the last.

On that June day, I met with the young boy who was severely injured and whose family was slaughtered a year before in the London truck attack. It was impossible to know the depths of agony he'd endured and would still. But he smiled as we spoke, and I saw that even the darkest hate can't destroy the joy of an innocent heart. He gave me hope that maybe rage and anger and fear can be defeated. Maybe.

I thought of all the vile comments and death threats that had been hurled at me just months before. There was no way I could truly know his pain. But I could feel a kind of kinship. There were people out there who hated us in the same way. I had seen that hate up close. I hadn't been harmed by it to anywhere near the degree he had, but I knew we were in this together.

Our joy eclipsed their hate.

I'd returned home to understand that part of my journey was learning that simple, beautiful fact. Of all the wonderful things my NHL career had brought me, the Stanley Cup included, the most important gift was that.

The parade began after our visit to the mosque. The parents and children who gathered there followed along as we rode triumphant through the streets of my hometown, hoisting the Cup as people lined the downtown streets and cheered.

And I proudly wore my "Too Many Men" t-shirt, which had become a bit of a viral sensation.

When I scored the game winning goal in Game 4 of the Stanley Cup final, there had been some whining about whether we had too many men on the ice. During the rush we botched our change and an extra player briefly stepped onto the ice. I'd picked up the puck in the neutral zone and was skating into their end, one-on-three. Our brief lapse had no effect on the play.

But after the game, Tampa's coach, Jon Cooper, was a little emotional and got pissed off about the play not being called. And fair enough, it was a huge swing game. That put up 3 games to one in the series, and it ended up leading us to the Stanley Cup.

A reporter later asked me about Jon's comments. They could tell I was stunned. I just kind of looked at them like it was the most absurd thing I'd ever heard. As soon as I heard it, I knew I had to make a t-shirt out of it if we won the Cup. I saw it as an opportunity to have some fun while raising money for a good cause.

I teamed up with a local designer and gave her a picture of our celebration after I scored. I asked her to come up with a concept for a t-shirt with the image and the words Too Many Men. She put together a great design and we managed to pull it all together in time for the parade. I wore it on stage as I hoisted the Cup for our fans.

The shirts were a huge hit. We'd set up a website and had a distributor ready to go. But we could hardly keep up with the orders. I didn't expect them to be that popular, but I think people in Denver are still wearing them to this day. We ended up raising $300,000 in sales, which all went to charity.

That day in London felt like the culmination of a long journey. So much lay ahead, but I'd reached a point in my career where I knew that I'd achieved what I'd set out to.

I was about to enter free agency for the first time.

I'd played some of the best hockey of my career that year. I ended up playing myself out of the Avalanche budget. I always hoped to stay with Colorado, but they had constraints with the current contract and the salary cap that pretty much made that impossible. It was just a reality of the business.

In a couple of months—after constant speculation, and more outside doubt as people believed I'd set the expectations of my value too high—I'd sign a seven-year $49 million contract to join the Calgary Flames.

I'd turn down great opportunities with the Islanders, Rangers, and Red Wings, to return to Canada, which meant so much to me. I'd start the final chapter in my hockey story in another city by the mountains, still playing on the edge, knowing that no one could take away what I'd already achieved.

But that was the future. That day, in London, I'd come home to remember where it started and why it mattered so much to me.

My family was there beside me, for this moment none of us could fully have fathomed. I held my grandfather close in my heart, and thanked him.

The parade carried us to Victoria Park, where hundreds more gathered around a bandshell. Several Lebanese flags waved alongside the maple leaf. The mayor presented me a key to the city. I stood at the dais, the Stanley Cup beside me. I leaned toward the mic.

"I'm hoping that this inspires and motivates kids to pursue your dreams because I never thought this was possible. I had some great support and people who made me believe," I told the crowd. "If you believe, you can achieve."

The crowd had gathered where the park's outdoor skating rink is built each winter. I looked across the wide seas of faces before me and saw a boy, shuffling on his edges, searching for balance.

ACKNOWLEDGMENTS

FROM NAZEM

Thank you to everyone who took time to read this book. I hope that you found it both entertaining and inspiring. Telling the story of my journey, which started with the hope and perseverance of my grandparents, has been a wonderful privilege.

Thank you to all my teammates and coaches who have helped make my career possible. I'm fortunate to have played alongside and for so many talented people.

I want to thank everyone who made this opportunity possible. To the entire team at Penguin Random House Canada, thank you for believing in the story that I wanted to share. Specifically, thank you to Nick Garrison for helping to bring this book to life.

Thank you to Rick Broadhead for your tireless work as my literary agent. And to Dan Robson for all of the hours we spent chatting and for capturing my story in these pages.

Most importantly, thank you to the family and friends who have inspired me and stood beside me all these years. To my parents and my sisters, thank you for your endless love and for being my biggest supporters. To Ashley and Naylah, thank you for being the best inspiration a man can hope for. Everything I have accomplished is because of the loved ones who helped make my dreams a reality. It's been a wonderful journey, so far—and I know the best days are still ahead.

FROM DAN

My enormous gratitude to everyone at Penguin Random House Canada for championing this story and all of the effort that went into making it come to life in these pages.

To Nick Garrison, thank you for your enthusiasm, support, and guidance as Nazem and I worked on his book. Thank you to Nicole Winstanley for believing in this project. Zainab Mirza, thank you for your patience and constant effort to help pull this project together. Thank you to Alanna McMullen for keeping us on track, despite me. And to Karen Alliston and Catherine Dorton for your meticulous work in making sure our book is as perfect as possible, also despite me.

Rick Broadhead, thank you as always for your exhaustive efforts as the best literary agent in the business.

To the Kadri family, thank you for the wonderful stories and insights you shared with me.

And finally, Nazem, thank you for the opportunity to help tell the story of your remarkable family and your unique journey to achieve extraordinary things. It's been a pleasure and an honour.

INDEX

A

Afzaal family (London truck
    attack), 195–96, 215
Aliu, Akim, 33, 35, 193, 195
Allen, Jake, 49
Amber, David, 213
American Hockey League. *See*
    specific teams
Andersen, Freddy, 172
Anderson, Craig, 76
Armstrong, Colby, 65
Azevedo, Justin, 27–28

B

Babcock, Mike, 135, 136–37, 139–42,
    146, 150–53
Backes, David, 161–62
Bäckström, Niklas, 133–34
Barbieri, Myles, 33
Barrie, Tyson, 181
Bednar, Jared, 189
Belleville Bulls, 26, 27–28
Belza, Anthony, 62

Bergeron, Patrice, 98, 104, 105
Binnington, Jordan, 202
Blake, Jason, 54
Bolland, Dave, 15
Boston Bruins, 75–76, 97–106
Boyle, Dan, 56
Bozak, Tyler, 66, 127, 135, 152, 166,
    171
Brodeur, Martin, 84
Bull Durham (film), 78, 82–83
Burke, Brian, 64–65, 67–68, 70, 72,
    79, 89–90
    and NK, 42–44, 47, 53, 82
Byram, Bowen, 206

C

Calgary Flames, 179–80, 217
Campbell, Jack, 50, 51
Canada Winter Games (2007), 21–22
Canadian Hockey League, 15. *See*
    also Memorial Cup; Ontario
    Hockey League
Carlson, John, 50

Carlyle, Randy, 84, 95, 100, 102, 130
    coaching style, 90–91, 120, 124
Carter, Jeff, 46
Cave, Ashley (Kadri), 164–65, 181
Chára, Zdeno, 98, 100, 104–5, 169,
    170, 173
Cherry, Don, 48, 71–72, 88, 96–97
Cogliano, Andrew, 202
Colborne, Joe, 79
Colorado Avalanche, 181, 183–89,
    212–13
    2019–20 season, 185–86, 191–92
    2020–21 season, 197–201
    2021–22 season, 201–12, 216
Cooper, Jon, 216
Crosby, Sidney, 16

D
Daley, Trevor, 195
Datsyuk, Pavel, 7–8, 140–41
DeBoer, Pete, 18, 25–26, 29, 95,
    164
DeBrusk, Jake, 172–73, 174
Del Zotto, Michael, 18, 21, 35–36
Desjardins, Willie, 49
Downie, Steve, 35
Dubas, Kyle, 172, 180–81
Duchene, Matt, 41, 42
Duclair, Anthony, 195
Dumba, Matt, 195

E
Eakins, Dallas, 73, 86–87
Eberle, Jordan, 49, 50, 51
Ekman-Larsson, Oliver, 41, 42
Ellis, Ryan, 41, 51

F
Faulk, Justin, 197–98
Franson, Cody, 103
Fraser, Matt, 132–33
Frattin, Matt, 79–80, 127, 139
Friedman, Elliotte, 213

G
Gardiner, Jake, 76, 84, 127, 135
Gatineau Olympiques, 27
Girardi, Daniel, 15
Giroux, Claude, 27
Grabovski, Mikhail, 66
Gunnarsson, Carl, 74, 104

H
Hagman, Niklas, 45
Halischuk, Matthew, 27, 28
Hall, Taylor, 37, 49, 51, 59
Hamilton, Ryan, 100
Hanson, Christian, 53
Hastings, Bobby, 54
Heatley, Dany, 56
Hedman, Victor, 40, 42, 94–95
Henrique, Adam, 21–22, 37, 49
hockey, 7, 10, 17–18. *See also*
    National Hockey League
    chirping in, 33, 46, 59, 156–59
    enforcers in, 157–58, 160
    power plays in, 155
    racism in, 11–12, 35, 63–64,
        192–95
Hockey Diversity Alliance, 194–95
Hockey Night in Canada, 96–97
Hodgson, Cody, 18, 22
Horachek, Peter, 130, 131, 134
Horton, Nathan, 104

Hunter, Dale, 15, 18, 26, 36, 124
Hunter, Dylan, 15
Hunter, Mark, 15, 18, 26
Husso, Ville, 206

J
Jágr, Jaromir, 98, 105
Johnson, Erik, 202, 205
Johnson, Jack, 202
Johnson, Tyler, 85
Jones, Martin, 49, 51

K
Kaberle, Tomáš, 54
Kadri, Ashley (née Cave), 164–65, 181
Kadri, Nazem (NK), 8–9, 16–18, 62–63. *See also specific teams*
  and celebrity, 48–49, 58–59, 128–29
  childhood and youth, 1, 2–3, 5–7, 15–17, 19–21, 31–32
  contract deals, 109–12, 135, 138, 145
  and criticism, 62–63, 65–66, 71–73, 81–82, 86–89, 110–11, 120–21, 199–201
  and failure, 121, 122–23
  family support (early career), 9–11, 17, 21, 30–31, 39–40, 43
  family support (in NHL), 55, 136–38, 200, 211, 213
  and fitness, 24, 62, 85–86, 88
  injuries, 33–35, 80, 201, 207–10
  in junior hockey, 21–22, 25, 29
  marriage and family, 164–66, 167, 181, 182, 183, 192

  and media, 121–22, 132
  in minor hockey, 8–11, 14, 16–17, 21
  as Muslim player, 40, 41, 47, 62–63, 193, 214–15
  and penalties, 155–56
  and racism, 11–12, 49–50, 193–96, 203–7, 215
  as smaller player, 8, 14, 16, 19–20, 47, 62
  Stanley Cup win, 211–12, 213, 214, 216–18
  suspensions, 131–34, 137, 157, 159–60, 170, 176–79, 198–201
Kadri, Nazem (grandfather), 3–4, 9, 23, 40, 112–16, 214
Kadri, Samir, 1–2, 115–16
  as father, 2, 6, 22–24, 214
  as supporter, 4–5, 10–11, 12, 43, 136–37
Kadri, Sharfi, 3, 114
Kadri, Sue, 5, 23–24, 43, 137
Kane, Evander, 41, 42
Kariya, Paul, 8
Kassian, Zack, 41
Kelly, Chris, 101
Kerfoot, Alex, 181
Kessel, Phil, 54, 66, 70–71, 90, 100, 103, 135
  hockey prowess, 76, 97, 101, 117, 126
  as teammate/mentor, 106, 127, 151, 161
Killorn, Alex, 85
King, Martin Luther, Jr., 123
Kitchener Rangers, 18–20, 24–29, 32–33, 36–37, 59–60

Komarov, Leo, 91, 166, 171
Kovalenko, Nikolai, 202
Kreider, Chris, 41
Krejčí, David, 98, 101, 104, 105
Kuemper, Darcy, 41
Kulemin, Nik, 96

L
Laine, Patrik, 146
Lamoriello, Lou, 136–39, 142–45,
    149–50, 171
Landeskog, Gabriel, 59, 184, 202
Lapierre, Maxim, 158
Latvia (World Junior
    Championships), 49
Lebanon, 3, 113, 114
Lecavalier, Vinny, 7–8
Leddy, Nick, 41
Lehkonen, Artturi, 202, 211
Loiselle, Claude, 72
London Junior Knights, 14
London Knights, 6–7, 14–16, 25
    2008–9 season, 30, 32–33, 34–38
    2009–10 season, 48, 53, 58,
        59–60
London (Ontario), 3, 6, 60, 214–16,
    217–18
Lucic, Milan, 98, 104, 105
Lupul, Joffrey, 76, 96, 127, 133

M
MacArthur, Clarke, 69–70, 91
MacKinnon, Nathan, 184, 185, 186,
    188, 202, 211
MacLean, Ron, 96–97
Makar, Cale, 184, 185–87, 202, 206
Marchand, Brad, 98, 106

Marleau, Patrick, 56, 162, 172
Marner, Mitch, 135, 139, 146, 147,
    151–52, 169
    as friend, 165, 167
    hockey prowess, 172, 186
Martin, Matt, 35
Mason, Steve, 25–26, 36
Matthews, Auston, 146–47, 165,
    172, 186
McLaren, Frazer, 91, 94, 97
McRae, Basil, 15
Memorial Cup (2008), 25, 27–29
Methot, Marc, 15
Minor Hockey Alliance of Ontario,
    14
Montreal Canadiens, 2, 90, 158
Murphy, Mike, 27, 28
Murray, Bryan, 43–44

N
Nabokov, Evgeni, 56, 95
National Hockey League (NHL). *See
    also* hockey; *specific teams*
    2009 draft, 38–44
    2012 lockout, 86
    2016 draft, 146–47
    2020 COVID shutdown, 191–92
    coaching styles, 124–25
    Department of Player Safety,
        133–34, 160, 173–75, 198
    fighting in, 91–93, 94–95, 160–64,
        167, 169–70, 201
    and mental health issues, 123–24
    old school *vs.* new school in,
        123–24, 152–53
    rookie players in, 47–48, 187
    team dynamics in, 166–67

Nonis, Dave, 111, 134
Norfolk Admirals, 85
Nylander, William, 139, 146, 147, 148, 165, 186

O
Ontario Hockey League, 15, 18, 21, 36–37. *See also specific teams*
O'Reilly, Ryan, 41
Orr, Bobby, 17
Orr, Colton, 91–94, 97, 127, 161
Ottawa Senators, 76

P
Palat, Ondrej, 85
Palmieri, Kyle, 41
Panik, Richard, 85
Perry, Corey, 15, 16
Peverley, Rich, 76
Phaneuf, Dion, 54, 101, 106, 126, 135, 139
    as team captain/mentor, 57, 76–77, 127, 132, 151, 161, 184
Pietrangelo, Alex, 21–22, 50, 51
Poulin, Dave, 72
Price, Carey, 90
Prust, Brandon, 15

Q
Quinn, Pat, 33–34

R
Ramage, John, 50
Rantanen, Mikko, 184, 205
Rask, Tuukka, 99, 100, 101, 103
Reimer, James, 76, 99, 101–2, 104, 127, 139

Rielly, Morgan, 135, 166
Roberts, Gary, 85, 87
Rosen, Calle, 181, 203

S
St. Louis, Marty, 63
Sakic, Joe, 183, 186
San Jose Sharks, 56
Schenn, Brayden, 41, 42, 49
Schenn, Luke, 76
Schremp, Rob, 15
Seguin, Taylor, 59
Sergachev, Mikhail, 210
Shanahan, Brendan, 130, 131–32, 134, 173
Silfverberg, Jakob, 41
Simmonds, Wayne, 195
Sjöström, Fredrik, 53
Skinner, Jeff, 59
Spalding, Nick, 28
Spokane Chiefs, 27, 28
Spott, Steve, 60
Stamkos, Steven, 18, 21–22, 210, 211
Stanley Cup
    2013 playoffs, 97–108, 117–18
    2022 finals, 208–12, 216
Stewart, Chris, 195
Switzerland (World Junior Championships), 49–50

T
Tampa Bay Lightning, 210, 211, 216
Tavares, John, 35–36, 40, 41–42, 172
Team Ontario (Canada Winter Games, 2007), 21–22
Thomas, Robert, 198

Thomas, Tim, 75–76
Thornton, Joe "Jumbo", 7–8, 56,
57, 162–64, 167
Tokarski, Dustin, 28
Toronto Maple Leafs, 42–44, 126–28,
181–82
2009–10 season, 45–48, 53–58
2010–11 season, 64–73, 74–77
2011–12 season, 78–80, 81–82
2012–13 season, 86–108, 117–18
2013–15 seasons, 117–18, 130–35
2015–16 season, 135–39, 141–44
2016–17 season, 146–53, 164
2017–19 seasons, 169–73, 176–79
Toronto Marlies, 67, 70, 73–74,
80–81, 84–85, 86–89

U
United States (World Junior
Championships), 50–52

V
Van Buskirk, Parker, 33
van Riemsdyk, James, 103, 117, 135,
166, 171
Vasilevskiy, Andrei, 210
Versteeg, Kris, 65
Višňovský, Ľubomír, 95
Vlasic, Marc-Édouard, 56

W
Ward, Joel, 195
Weber, Shea, 16
Wideman, Dennis, 15
Wilson, Jason, 33, 35
Wilson, Ron, 55, 57–58, 74, 77, 84
as coach, 65–66, 75, 79, 124
Windsor Spitfires, 37–38
Wingels, Tommy, 169–70
World Junior Championships,
33–34, 49–52